Winston L. Shelton
...a life of Invention

as told to
Steve Coomes

with contributions from
Valerie Shelton & William Arbaugh

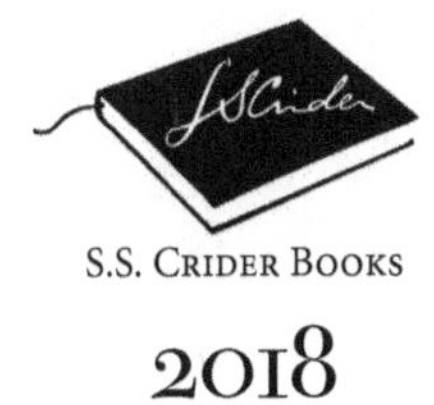

S.S. CRIDER BOOKS

2018

ISBN: 978-0-692-99184-8

10 9 8 7 6 5 4 3 2 1

1. Biography

First Edition

Contents

Dedication

"We dedicate this book to Winston L. Shelton, who continues to answer his father's charge to improve the world through insight, invention and effort."

– the Authors

"My Paper"

INTRODUCTION

Winston L. Shelton

It's been said that a "prepared mind" naturally attracts opportunities it can manage and master due to its prolonged exposure to the forces of time and circumstance.

Or, perhaps more simply put, we are very much products of our upbringing and the experiences we've gained throughout our lives. And I believe, wholeheartedly, that when we act positively with the knowledge we've gained along the way, amazing things can happen.

I like to think that growing up with so many junkyard machine parts and just a few store-bought toys helped me become mechanically minded and, eventually, a successful inventor.

I'm also confident my parents' insistence that I and my siblings did well in school prepared me to be a suitable student when delivered to Princeton University—without warning and by direct order of the U.S. Army, I might add. I couldn't have envisioned either of those events and many others on the horizon of my life, but when introduced to those situations, I seemed able to thrive in them. I wish I could say I recognized them then as the gifts they were, but looking back on them now, it's clear I was terrifically fortunate.

That's partly why I've worked to write down some recollections of the life that's been mine for the past 95 years. It wasn't as though I wanted to write a book. My daughter, Valerie Shelton, the CEO of Winston Industries, the company I founded almost 50 years ago, has insisted for years that the stories of my days be told to others—not for my sake, but theirs. She believes strongly that others can benefit from my experiences and perhaps enjoy a few laughs along the way.

So, I've acceded to telling what I can recall, sharing what I regard as most beneficial to others. I must admit that, when first asked to write of my life experiences in the form of a book, it felt very much like an assignment from a tyrant teacher whose greatest joy is the misery of others. It felt much like a return to childhood when given "a paper" to write. As an engineer for 69 years, I'm more at ease discussing how things work and imagining how to make them better.

I'm not reluctant to revisit the past or talk about myself, for my life has been an adventure full of discovery, incredible friendships and experiences. Perhaps my attitude toward this endeavor comes down to my preference to look forward and envision what's left for persons such as myself to do, rather than look backward. Or maybe it's just this simple: The exercise of chronicling it sounds like work!

Regardless, the assignment is before me, and I'll finish it. To begin it, I searched inside myself for the subject material, and as one my age can attest, there's a lot to draw on. In fact, I can attribute the direction to, in essence, make my life worthy of a story as coming from my father. In my youth, my father would frequently invite me to take road trips with him. Be it deer hunting, a business trip, a basketball game and more, those trips lasted the span of a weekend or sometimes longer.

In our travels, we shared thoughts as do most when confined to an automobile for extended periods, but mostly we enjoyed being with each other, even when long silences settled upon our conversations. Often, a response to a question was so delayed that the original question was forgotten. In remembering those times, I'd like to think we were just deep in thought—happily there, in fact.

During one road trip, I asked Dad what he would have done with his life had he had the chance to change it. Sometime later, much later—long after I had forgotten the question—he said, "What I really have wanted to do was make the lives of all others better by reason of my being here."

I can't say I was expecting that answer. But there it was, hanging in the space between us, and perhaps heavily so on the mind of a teenager who couldn't yet fully gauge its profundity. Yet his statement never left me as I considered it over and over. As I grew and could better comprehend its meaning with every passing year, it became clear that he had given me, albeit implicitly, an assignment to do the same—to make others' lives better.

Once I grasped the seriousness of what he said, that thought began to consume my life. How those efforts manifested themselves were often as much a surprise to me as anyone.

Now, just months shy of my 96th birthday, I am forced to hand in "my paper," and in so doing examine whether I lived up to my father's lofty aim.

The truth about self-analysis is it's a difficult thing to perform with any measurable accuracy—which happens to be the very essence of what I do as an engineer. The journey down the road of personal assessment is fraught with distortions of ego, time, perceived vs. actual benefits conveyed to others, etc. And any such trip backward tends to expose the myriad human shortcomings that can leave us with a perilously loose grasp on the truth. In other words, it's just as easy to fool oneself into thinking he's done better than he has as it is to short-change oneself by under-evaluating the positive contributions he's made.

What this "assignment" has taught me is serendipity was primarily in charge of my life, while others influenced it profoundly as well. (So how can I take credit for either?)

I refer to my youthful assignments given by Mother in her kitchen (she let me play with her tools, mashing onions into potatoes, etc.), and my practical assignments that led to the Army changing my career direction from law to engineering. I'd have never envisioned how my work at General Electric would lead me to a relationship with "Colonel" Harland Sanders and the subsequent creation of a pair of groundbreaking restaurant industry devices that, to my way of thinking, really have made others' lives better.

Perhaps it's just time to submit "my paper" and let you, dear reader, decide for yourself.

— Winston Shelton, 2017

Humble Beginnings

WEST VIRGINIA DAYS

I come from humble beginnings.

My father, Naaman Shelton, Sr., was born in 1889 in Nicholas County, West Virginia, and was one of eleven children. His father owned a horse-drawn hauling service that provided the family a modest, but respectable income. My mother, Opal Dell (Keenan) Shelton, was born in 1895, had eight siblings and was the daughter of a casket maker. Both grew up in Nicholas County, West Virginia, and on March 24, 1912, they married.

Their union produced six offspring and 92 first cousins. And while they began their lives together more than a century ago, their determination and resilience is still alive and well in myself, my children, and my grandchildren, and my hope is that it will be passed on for many more generations.

I was born Winston Laverne Shelton on May 3, 1922, in Lockwood, West Virginia, the youngest of my parents' five children. My

A typical 1920s West Virginia lumber camp readying saw logs to be hoisted onto rail cars.

"age of recollection" began when I was just shy of 3. Like my parents, my family lived in Nicholas County in a four-room home beside Peters Creek. (I remember hearing Dad say our home was "about 8 miles below Summersville," if you prefer more precision.) Some doubt my ability to recall events from such a young age, but my memory of my younger brother Billy's death just 11 hours after his birth convinces me otherwise.

Our home on Peters Creek was located conveniently between the Richwood and Swiss lumber camps, which represented employment for Dad. Our family of seven slept in two of the four rooms—Mother, Dad and me in one bedroom, and my three sisters, Ann, Olive and Clytice, and Naaman Jr., my older brother, in the other bedroom.

Our house had every convenience of the modern households of the 1920s: a "john" situated just outside the back door, cold running water from a spring about 50 yards from the house, a wash tub in which to bathe in the kitchen, and kerosene lamps for lighting. For the kids, modern transportation consisted of walking every place one needed to go. Dad, however, had a Ford Model T truck that had but one purpose: to take him to work in a lumber camp on Monday and return him home each Friday.

Instead of a fuel pump, the old Ford had a gravity-fed fuel tank that proved suitable until meeting a steep incline—a common problem in mountainous West Virginia. That placed the engine higher than the fuel tank, which meant the engine could get no fuel. Backing up steep inclines (a mountain in our case), solved the problem by elevating the fuel tank above the engine.

Groceries came from our cow, our garden and a country store up the road about half a mile. The cow generously provided milk and butter, and the orchard we shared with my Uncle John Shelton provided apples and peaches for our family and his. Jars and jars of apple butter were canned by Mother and the girls, and to this day, I still delight in the deliciousness provided by the thick brown concoction.

There were only four or five houses in Peters Creek, and one of those belonged to my Uncle John and Aunt Georgia Shelton. We lived within "hollering distance" of both their house and blacksmith shop, which was just across the road. Uncle John was Dad's brother and Aunt Georgia was Mother's sister. Their four children, Katy, Billy, Agnes and Vina Mae therefore were "double first cousins" to us.

This community of Sheltons within sight of one another is surely what allowed my father the ability to work in the lumber camps during the week. Living and thriving in Peters Creek required families to be self-reliant and resourceful, yet cooperative and interdependent at the same time.

My beloved "Uncle" Tommy Williams, owner and editor of the *Clay County Free Press*, was really just a close friend of the family, as well as "uncle" to many other children in the community.

The rest of the family told me he had given me a horse named Prancer, but I never saw Prancer or received any compensation from his sale or disposal. The story was that Prancer was being kept by my Uncle Winston Shelton in Clay, but even after we moved there, Prancer eluded me. I always suspected that Prancer had a great many other owners — all of whom were the "nieces" and "nephews" of good ol' "Uncle" Tommy.

Brown sugar in a barrel in the aisle of a general store is what 4-year-olds dreamed about in those days. Standing tippy-toed, I reached downward from the crook in my arm to the sugar, and wonderful things happened. As my fingers sifted through the sugar, I inevitably encountered lumps. Sifting the lumps, I would usually find one of a "proper" size—that is, a sugar lump that would last a good part of the day and maybe into bedtime. Pure bliss.

A formidable opponent to my youth at Peters Creek was our horned milk cow, Bossie. Playing at the spring meant crossing into her territory.

A trip to the spring with my brother Naaman Jr., made for safe travel, but I feared going alone. It would be sometime in the future before I would be any match for Bossie, as any confrontation would surely mean she would have the last word if she separated me from the others.

Headed away from Bossie was a chestnut tree that provided an essential lesson about good things in life: Sometimes we can't see the good through the bad, and often, when things seem the worst, we just haven't uncovered the good yet.

Here's why: The outer shell of every chestnut is covered in very sharp spiny burrs. The shell is as imposing a threat to one's satisfaction of the chestnut as Bossie was to my going to the spring. And it's not just the burr surrounding the chestnut; it is last season's burrs now buried in the grass. Their spiny lances protect the territory around the tree against bare feet. Collecting and opening the chestnuts requires well-soled shoes, thick leather gloves and an infinite amount of patience as one waits for the few weeks when the chestnuts are their tastiest.

The Shelton family's Cross Roads Restaurant and Service Station in Two Run, West Virginia.

CLAY, WEST VIRGINIA

I remember the trip that moved us from Nicholas County to Clay, West Virginia, in 1925; Dad had accepted a job as a mechanic working for my Uncle Winston. We arrived in the night and moved into a three-room house Dad had rented. While the new quarters were more cramped than those in Nicholas County, there were real benefits to the new home. It was just beside Mr. Cruikshank's hardware store and his dump, which provided myriad large boxes allowing us to build a village of "houses." The stuff he threw into his dump represented everything my brother and I needed to furnish our houses. Also, the house was just across the street from Mr. Sizemore's general store: a closer source for the brown sugar that was inevitably marketed from a whiskey barrel.

When I was only 4, I started going to Clay County Grade School when my brother Naaman Jr., started at age 6. Gus Andrews was the teacher and school principal.

After I'd been there a few days, he came to call on Mother and Dad, saying he wanted to enroll me in the school. He felt I was able to attend and do the work, plus, he convinced my parents I would be much less trouble as a student instead of being my brother's guest each day. It was a four-room schoolhouse—the first and second grades were in one room, third and fourth in another, fifth and sixth and seventh and eighth in two others.

My enrollment in school surely allowed Dad and Mother the freedom of developing some land they had purchased in 1926. At the junction of routes 4 and 16 at Two Run, they built a restaurant and service station and named it Cross Roads Restaurant and Service Station. The three-level structure, financed by local banker Sam McClain, also would become our home, where we moved to in 1927. Along with personnel hired to work at the business, I lived there until I went to Glenville College (West Virginia) in 1941.

The structure's bottom level matched the elevation of the bottom land just above the nearby Elk River, which, on its torturous course through the mountains, flooded frequently. The next level was our living quarters, which were built into the grade of the hill. That meant half of the rooms in the lower levels had no windows as they abutted the side of the hill. The third level met the level of the road, so that space was used for the restaurant and service station. The lot sloped behind the building, slanting down in the back as it fell off toward the river. Mother and Dad's enterprise would soon become the best retail business in the county.

In the second grade, I left Clay County School to attend Two Run Grade School. While I was in that school, I moved from the second grade all the way to the fifth grade within that one school year. Because of that, I was suddenly a student on the same level as my older brother, Naaman Jr., who wasn't all that pleased with that turn of events.

My brother was, of course, physically much larger and stronger. He was also very clever. My being placed in his class, even though I was three school grades younger, was a disaster, and he was understandably critical of me. My answer to that was to study and work harder than he did. In order to "earn my place" among the older students, my achievements were scholastic.

During fifth grade, my parents were involved in a struggle at the school over the appointment of a teacher they didn't want leading the class. When the teacher they preferred wasn't chosen, I, Clytice and Naaman Jr., were then placed in Spread School, but our time there was brief due to the inconvenience of getting there. Located more than five miles up the road, our teacher would pick up me and my siblings on his way to the school. After about two weeks, that arrangement was deemed too complicated and we ended up going back to Clay County Grade School.

On our first day back, someone picked a fight with Naaman Jr., and our sister Clytice whipped the oppressor. After that, everyone in the school regarded the Shelton kids as real "tough guys," and gave us a wide berth. Though I hadn't been involved in the skirmish, I did enjoy the notoriety. A boy in my class, Garrett Davis, was scared of me, and all I had to do was raise my hand near him as if I was going to strike him and he would flinch and cower. Ironically, we ended up being the best of friends.

Overall, I liked going back to Clay. The building was brick, and there was a large play yard with swings, a merry-go-round and a see-saw. I enjoyed the Ginn & Company readers, history books and arithmetic books. I liked school and was typically the winner of spelling bees. We sometimes had spelling bees on Fridays if everyone had gotten their work done during the week. I finished the 8th grade there just after my 11th birthday.

I was only 12 when I started attending Clay High School in 1933. I did all of my homework and enjoyed English and Poetry. I can still recite "The House by The Side of the Road," by Sam Walter Foss, and many other poems I memorized.

I stayed there only a year because my parents sent Naaman Jr., to Greenbrier Military School in 1934, and I got to join him there in 1935. My brother was sent to the military school in an effort to help him "appreciate rules" (one example why follows later in this book). I went simply because I wanted to be with my brother. Again, I passed him in school performance, which he later seemed to resent. I was, after all, three years younger than him, and he was still stronger than me as well as very bright as a student. Our being in school together, and our being brothers, meant many made unfair comparisons between the two of us. Whether his leaving high school before graduation was an outcome of that, I don't know.

I stayed at Greenbrier until 1937, but then returned to Clay High in the fall at the request of Coach O. R. Baker, who wanted Naaman Jr., and me to play football there. The football program had been interrupted for a few years because of a fatal injury suffered by one of its players in a game.

THE RESTAURANT

My parents' Cross Roads Restaurant featured a counter with stools; three booths; and a few tables for customer accommodation. Later, a private room was added for family dining and for weekly events concerning the Clay Rotary Club and Lions Club.

Winston's mother,
Opal Keenan Shelton.

Mother was up every day at 5 a.m., while Naaman Jr., and I got up at 7 a.m. on school days and slept until 8 a.m. in the summer. When we got up, the morning restaurant breakfast rush was over.

Often, we would make our own pancakes for breakfast since the ladies Mother hired were very busy cooking in the morning. We eventually became unafraid of anything in the kitchen. There was no one in that household who couldn't go to a stove and prepare a meal. That's one way Mother taught us: by having us do it.

In that restaurant, Mother was the very example of determination. She had five ladies reporting to her (who also roomed with us), and she had five children in the same household she cared for. She learned to do that by cooking with her own mother at a lumber camp—which is where she met Dad. That experience made her a very disciplined worker.

Mother was very strong on manners. She taught us that when a customer came through that door, even if you were busy, you looked up and smiled. Even if you had nothing particular to communicate to them, you were supposed to let them know this was a happy place to be. Once, she saw one of the ladies we had working for us who'd failed to do that, and oh, boy, Mother had a lecture for her. She wanted the people who came to our place to eat to be comfortable.

Since we were located at a crossroads, we had customers come there from all over the country. That exposed Mother to people of higher culture, especially those who had a nice way of speaking. She took notice that they were more cosmopolitan. She taught us to respect travelers and understand that by being with them, they were teaching us.

The restaurant was known for its pies: blackberry with a solid crust, the top pierced with a knife to allow steam to escape, mincemeat and pumpkin, custard and lemon topped with meringue, and apple with a crisscross lattice crust. Mother had a three-sided, glass-walled pie safe, where she displayed her slices of pie and cake on white plates.

The berries for those pies were picked and delivered by Cleve Drake's family, who would stop by and pick up Mother's 5-gallon lard buckets saved for the occasion. Mr. Drake was married to Ocie Drake, who had three children, Downton, Helen and Gertrude.

The restaurant served sandwiches at lunch—always on Holsum or

Purity Maid white sandwich bread—and made thusly: ham; ham and cheese; and fried egg (from our chickens tended by me and my brother).

Mother's original coal stove was replaced by a kerosene stove, which was quickly replaced with a gasoline stove because the kerosene exhaust made the biscuits and food taste like burned oil. When the gasoline stove caused a fire, it was replaced with a natural gas stove. There were natural gas fields throughout the region, and many folks had their own oil rigs with which they pumped both oil and natural gas. Natural gas was so abundant that many just burned it off rather than store it. (My brother was quite clever and devised a way to capture "white gas" condensate from natural gas, which he used to power his vehicles.)

The local health inspector required a health certificate for every restaurant worker, checking for tuberculosis and other diseases as well as their general health. Mother always earned an "A" rating, having made sure every employee had been checked and had passed.

Mother had most of her restaurant supplies and groceries delivered by a purveyor. Her meat was ordered a week in advance, while other groceries were bought by Mother in town, using our family truck, a 1927 Ford Model A pickup.

There were no refrigerators when my parents started the restaurant. I remember ice being delivered on a truck for Mother's restaurant long before her cooler was converted into an electrically refrigerated cooler. She used to place a small, square cardboard sign in the window to order ice. Each side of the square had a different number: 10, 20, 50, etc., indicating the total poundage of ice you needed. The ice came on a truck owned by the Diamond Ice Company of Charleston, West Virginia.

Lunch at the restaurant was served from a steam table brimming with vegetables that included green beans, buttered, boiled potatoes, corn (roasting ears in season), beets (I don't like beets!), turnips, carrots, green onions, cabbage and the like. The meats served at lunch included pot roast, roast beef, pork and meatloaf. I don't remember any chicken on the menu.

Of course, we ate the same food served to the restaurant's customers. There were a series of weekly and monthly meetings at the restaurant (Lions Club, Ladies' Auxiliary Club, Rotary Club) and all these meetings had special dinner menus from which we ate, too. My favorite meal growing up was fried pork chops and fried potatoes.

I can still remember each of the waitresses recounting the menu at the counter: "Ham, hamburger, cheese, eggs, ham and eggs sandwiches, also plate lunches, 35 cents … from the steam table."

The restaurant served Maxwell House coffee. (Since I didn't start drinking coffee until I was an adult, I can't attest to its quality. I was working at G.E. when I began drinking coffee, because it proved to be a convenient way to socialize at work. I was amused to learn G.E. didn't use G.E. coffee makers, instead they used Bunn-O-Matic coffee stations).

The restaurant had a Western Electric crank handle telephone, and our party line phone number was 7. In order to call our house, the caller had to crank the phone handle with "one long crank (which caused one long ring) and two short cranks (two short rings)," to dial the "7."

The house and restaurant had running water as well as indoor plumbing and toilets. While water coming to the house wasn't potable, my father had devised a water pump on the side of the hill in back of the house that pumped river water from the creek branch into a holding well. It was a wooden tank with a gravity feed to the station and house. We eventually had treated city water when the city built a water pumping station. The city water was purified and had a noticeable taste of chlorine.

We had six bathrooms available for the folks who lived in the house. Two were conveniently next to the service station, two were for the restaurant and two in the house for the hired help and family. If you went to one and it was locked, you simply went to the next.

Since the family lived at the restaurant, all of us were pressed into some duty at different times. Of course, school was the first priority, so Mother needed full-time outside help with the restaurant and Dad needed similar male help with the service station. My Aunt Claura and Uncle Edgar Keenan were hired first, followed by Virgie Butcher in the kitchen and first cousin Bud Shelton for the service station. Family duties were plentiful after school and on weekends. My own much-coveted duty was mashing potatoes for Mother. In this case, I was given creative latitude to chop onions and mix them into the potatoes.

Incidentally, the restaurant was where I began a highly irregular habit of smoking cigarettes around age 7. Cigarettes were sold at the restaurant, and I suppose that, as a child, I was curious and picked one or two off the ground that someone hadn't finished but casually discarded. When I grew older, perhaps 12 or 13, someone told me that if I wanted to be an athlete, I couldn't smoke. Well, I listened to that because I wanted to play football! I never smoked much anyway, so when I gave up my monthly cigarette when I was 13, it wasn't all that significant.

To provide a little perspective, our business had only one competitor close by. A Mr. Poole ran the Standard Oil service station within sight of our station, but his number of customers seemed to match his reduced level of service. Probably the decision maker for a potential gasoline customer was whether one preferred Gulf or Standard Oil's Esso fuel.

Clay was two miles away (and was the county seat for Clay County), and it boasted a Shell gas station, the Clay County Bank, three grocery stores, two dry goods stores, a hardware store, a movie house for Saturday night and a jewelry store. Of course, the Clay County Court House and Jail had a solid place in the community, as did the grade school and high school. Two churches were in existence, Baptist and Methodist. What else did one need? The population of the town of Clay in 1930 was just 444. As a whole, according to the United States Census Bureau, the county was home to 13,000 back then. As of 2010, the Census said the county was closer to 9,300.

THE GREAT DEPRESSION

We didn't much feel the effects of the Depression. We were fortunate because we dealt in two necessary commodities: gasoline and food. People simply had to have them.

Dad and Mother would always feed hungry people who could not pay at the restaurant. One thing I remember were the number of people on the side of the road hitchhiking. They were trying to find work and knew they needed to go someplace else. Employment in our part of the world was primarily coal mining and timber cutting; there were really no other jobs to be had. A few folks traded for a living, running a dry-goods or another type of small store.

Winston's father, Naaman Shelton, Sr.

I remember Dad often telling me to "go out and ask those people sitting along the side of the road on the stone wall to come in and have dinner with us." And they would.

I also remember a train car pulling into the Clay County rail depot on the rail siding. They pulled the gates open on the side of the car and handed out white sacks of food to the folks who had lined up. The rail siding was about two miles up from our gas station and restaurant, and you would see a stream of men walking past our station carrying their sacks. Many made 8- and 10-mile round trips on foot to get those sacks.

The handouts were part of Roosevelt's National Recovery Act, a.k.a., the NRA. We also had a number of other federal projects in the area under the auspices of the Works Progress Administration (WPA). Young men would work converting dirt roads into gravel roads, breaking limestone boulders into gravel, building bridges and other infrastructure. The young men were given an Army-like uniform and paid $8 per month. Their families received $8 a month as well.

Some young men in the area were recruited into the Civilian Conservation Corps (CCC), building federal structures and tending national parks and the like. I remember one local group was sent to Racine, Wisconsin, where they built a post office. With the start of the Second World War, however, all that federal assistance ended.

Naaman Shelton Sr.'s Gulf gas station as seen through the front window of the Cross Roads Restaurant.

Gasoline Dealer

My father, Naaman Sr., started out as a Standard Oil / Esso gasoline dealer. He had a falling out with the company and switched to selling Gulf Oil gasoline. The service station had an area called the "oil room," where vehicles were lubricated, had their oil changed, etc. That's where a lot of the auto repair took place. I didn't have to maintain any of the equipment or machinery; the workers at the service station did all of that.

We had Tokheim gas pumps, which were equipped with a 5-gallon glass globe tank at the top. You had to hand pump the gas upward and into the globe and then open a release valve to let gravity drain the pump to fill the customer's gas tank.

As soon as Naaman Jr., and I got old enough, pumping gas for customers was a chore given to us. In the winter we didn't have to do it because of school, but in the summer it was our daily job. For our service, we earned 15 cents each morning and afternoon. When I became a paid worker, I seem to remember some discussion about how that would eliminate my up-to-then free ice cream and candy account in the restaurant.

The Sawmill

In addition to the service station, Dad also owned and operated a sawmill usually employing 10 to 12 workers at a time. A man named "Greasy" Jones (Newman Wilson Jones) had two sons, Firpo (Donald Romie Jones) and Casey (Hazleton Richard Jones). A family full of nicknames! Firpo and I became fast friends. Dad had hired his father, Greasy, away from the Elk River Coal and Lumber Company. He was our "mill hand" (a millwright) and was the nominal supervisor of Dad's sawmill.

I still remember Greasy wearing my football cleats throughout our family's house after he'd worn them that day, working in the sawmill. That caused some pandemonium given Mother's insistence on a clean house—a tall order given the number of people living there! Dad didn't mind a little disarray, but they worked together and everything ended up just fine.

Holidays: Halloween

My brother and I would make the 2-mile walk to Clay for Halloween, and we'd start by soaping windows with bars of Ivory or Fels-Naptha, whatever soap Mother had around the house. Another fun thing to do was to set a pile of newspapers on fire on someone's door stoop, ring the doorbell, run away and watch them come out and stomp out the fire. We'd light paper bags full of shit on fire, too, just for fun. Believe it or not, my brother and I were pretty well controlled compared to some.

We'd get some candy on Halloween, but we were much more interested in performing "tricks" than we were in getting "treats." We would run down the streets with a long stick, scraping it along the iron bars or the wooden pickets of a fence, just to hear the sound in the night. We celebrated Halloween in a much more contained way at school.

Holidays: Christmas & Easter

Despite it being Christmas, we were always open for business. The restaurant itself was decorated nicely, and the Christmas tree, which was in the private dining room, included gifts underneath it for everybody. As I remember, my brother and I would get things like high-top boots and sleds for Christmas.

It wasn't as busy as a typical day at the restaurant, but there were many who came—a large public family, really. Special friends also would drop in because the restaurant was open. Some who stopped by on Christmas were in awe of the party they'd happened upon.

The Easter Bunny always visited during the night before Easter. He'd leave new clothes, candy and dyed eggs at the foot of our beds and we'd discover his treats upon awakening Easter morning.

Church

My parents were Southern Baptists. We all attended the local Baptist church when we were little. I went to Bible School. Later, the Bomont Methodist Church in Clendenin burned down, and the community built a new church in its place, one that included a gymnasium. So, my brother and I started attending the new Methodist church so we could use the gym.

My mom and dad were very happy about our "conversion" to Methodism because some folks in town were partial to those who attended Baptist services and some were partial to those who attended Methodist services—and consequently the restaurant business grew because of our family's expanding religious affiliations. I attended Methodist Sunday School and had a Methodist "water sprinkle" baptism. I don't remember if I had been baptized earlier in the Baptist church. Both sets of ministers would often come to call and partake of supper, and that's the only time I remember our family saying "Grace." We did it to keep up appearances for the visiting ministers.

DAILY LIFE

I shared a room with Naaman Jr., until I was 15 when I was told I could have my own room. In my room, I built a cabinet with left-over construction materials: V-groove pine boards and other lumber. I stored my trinkets and personal effects in my cabinet. However, I built the cabinet to have a false bottom where I stored my "secrets." The cabinet door was made of beadboard with rails and stiles and a diagonal cross-member to give the door structural rigidity.

To have electric light in the evening, the family had to turn on our International Harvester electric generator, which ran on natural gas. But since the generator caused radio wave interference, we had to use a battery to power a tall Crosley console radio. We listened to Lowell Thomas' news broadcast at 6:30 p.m., followed by Amos & Andy at 6:45. By then the battery was fading and the radio was switched off and the generator could once again provide electric light. We listened to the programs on Pittsburgh radio station KDKA, which was founded by the Westinghouse Electric Corporation in 1920.

Mom drove herself to the stores in town in our black Model A Ford pickup. It cost $495 new. That would cost $8,900 in 2017.

My dad taught me to drive whenever we'd go anyplace. He'd put me in his lap behind the steering wheel and let me steer. I would often oversteer because I wanted to make sure I got around the curve. Dad would grab the wheel and correct my efforts, saying "Don't oversteer, son."

We bought our clothes from Blanch Pearson at a dry goods store in Clay. Generally, clothes were purchased once a year, before the upcoming school term. I wore overalls with a blue chambray work shirt. The shirt doubled as a sleeping shirt or night gown. I took a bath every Saturday.

The first time I remember having a suit must have been an early outfit with knickers, when I was about 10 years old. The knickers were made of heavy wool. That outfit, my first "grown up" suit, surely came from Frankenberger's, over in Charleston, a place for fine clothing for men and boys. I remember the outfit was a soft, gray tweed. My mother had put my sister Olive in charge of my dress, which was my good fortune. Olive was always so neat in her appearance, and since she had studied Home Economics, she made her own clothes extremely well, I might add. Olive was certainly the one who helped me into my new little suit with knicker pants. I even had a bow tie to complete my outfit. But since, at 10, I hadn't yet learned how to tie a bow tie, it was fitted with a snap.

I had started buying my own clothes around the age of 15, which I deemed important given that two of my friends were girls: Nancy Friend and Catherine Jones. I'd started driving a truck (you were able to get your driver's license at 15 in West Virginia at that time) for my dad's business and I'd earned some money. I went to Frankenberger's and selected a green tweed suit with a white shirt and a colorful tie. I got dressed up in my new suit, drove over to Nancy's and stopped in front of her house. She came out, and I opened the door so she could see my suit. I sat there for a few moments while she looked at me and then I drove away.

Once, Dad said he needed somebody to drive a truck to Pittsburgh to pick up a machine, and he turns to me and says, "You just got your license, right?" Mother said no, but he said yes, so I took some NoDoz (a high-caffeine "energy" pill) and drove through the night to Pittsburgh. It was about a 300-mile drive back then. I got the machine and then drove back that same day.

My father was great at letting us learn on the job. He always had us fixing things even though we didn't know how. But he knew the best thing he could do for us was let us take it apart, recognize the problem, fix it and put it back together. You didn't call a mechanic back then, you did the job yourself. When we got in trouble, he helped us. He allowed us to fail because he knew that by failing you succeed in learning.

Favorite Treats

I loved candy bars: Clark, Baby Ruth, Snickers and Heath English Toffee. I often ate them in the car when I was riding to town with Mother. I was allowed a daily allotment of a candy bar, an ice cream and a soft drink. These were sold by the bottle from a water-cooled Coke cooler in the service station. My favorite soft drinks were Coca-Cola and Nehi Chocolate. These were bottled locally at the Charleston Bottling Co.

Since I was youngest in the family, I was often jerked from school to go with Mother into town to get the things for the restaurant that hadn't been delivered. We would always stop by the Charleston Bottling Co., where I was allowed a bottle of soda.

When Mother was in town on business, she would sometimes send me to the movie at the Roxy Theatre, telling me where in the theater to sit. When she finished her business, she'd come in, find me and we'd go. I didn't really care for the popcorn you could get at the movie theater.

Dating

At 15, I started dating Nancy Friend. We'd take my red bicycle to the movie theater in town. She rode on the handlebars. She and I were tennis partners at the tennis courts downtown, but I wasn't very good at tennis. Later, I started taking Nancy to the movies on Fridays in the family truck. For a dollar, I could buy two movie tickets, two milkshakes and a couple of gallons of gas for the truck.

I loved the movies. I liked "Gone with The Wind," cowboys like "The Lone Ranger," "The Northwest Passage," "The Crusades" and cowboy actor Tom Mix. I always sat in the front row so no one could block my view.

CHILDHOOD & EARLY TEENS

In pre-teens and teens, my brother and I were constantly "doing things" that I doubt many people would agree were worthwhile. But to us, it was a valuable education for our much-later careers. We did many things our friends never attempted.

We were allowed to use Dad's tools, in spite of the fact that they usually ended up in wet grass with a lot of rust on them. Naaman Jr., being older and bigger, was the boss of the projects and the better doer. He made me the person who had to fetch everything. He'd say, "Go get me a this … go get me a that … go get me some more of …" something he needed.

I remember that our tool selection included a hammer, a saw and an auger with a few drill bits. If we couldn't find a tool to do the job, we simply did it another way. Drilling holes in wood was no problem at all, even if we didn't have the right size drill. We discovered a hot poker would allow us to drill any size hole we wished.

My brother and I had a bicycle without a rear wheel, and how we acquired that bicycle, I don't know—but I don't think we stole it! We needed a rear wheel for it, and we didn't have the money to buy one, so we found a wooden-spoked automobile wheel that we altered to fit the yoke of the bike. We then affixed a coaster brake to it. It wasn't perfect, but we had a bicycle and we rode that thing! We were about 10 or 12 when we made it.

A friend, Frankie Bishop had a Maytag gasoline-powered washing machine motor, and we bought that from him for $3. So now we had a motor we could drive things with. The first project was an attempt to put it on a boat. We bought a propeller some place, or maybe we talked our uncle out of it. We bought a water pump drive, and since the service station was doing mechanical work, we found a water pump (which we didn't take from any car!) and we mounted it to a propeller. We then mounted it on the prow of the boat on a couple of bed rails. The gasoline washing machine motor was a V-belt drive and we used it to turn the propeller. Well, it worked grandly in the air, but in the water, we had a V belt entering and exiting the water and throwing water everywhere. We could never go more than 20 feet before the water wetted the spark plug and we stopped.

We then took the motor off the boat to make a little car using a wagon. We had a good selection of fan belts at the service station, so we put a belt around the pulley and then around a wheel of the wagon—making the belt, effectively, the tire. We started the engine with the wheel in the air, then let it down and it would go forward. We had a little steering wheel on it. We could drive around the service station. As long as we were on black top or concrete it was great. It didn't work so well in the grass.

One time we created a diving helmet and used it to walk underwater on the bottom of the Elk River. We took a 5-gallon lard bucket and cut two shallow scoops on opposite sides of the bucket. These were notches for our shoulders when we turned the bucket upside down and plopped it on our heads. We padded the cut edges of the bucket with lengths of garden hose cut along the long side of the hose pieces so the bare metal wouldn't cut into our shoulders. We attached twine to the bucket and tied the twine under our arms so it wouldn't float off our heads because of the air inside when we were underwater.

We cut a window in the front of the upside-down bucket and fitted a piece of isinglass (in this case, a thin sheet of mica, probably taken from a lantern or kerosene heater) so we could look around in our new underwater world.

In our first test, we discovered we were too buoyant to walk along the bottom of the river when we wore our diving helmet. Our solution? We just grabbed a 10-pound rock and carried it in our arms as we waded into the river. Success! About the time we were halfway across the river, we would run out of air. We'd drop the rock and shoot to the surface. We later used a bicycle pump and a hose attached to the bucket to lengthen our stay underwater. Whoever was not underwater pumped the bicycle pump, allowing the underwater explorer a longer trip. Dad interrupted the process when we said we planned to use a compressor in order to stay under water indefinitely.

One day, an old truck died at the gas station, and our workers merely pushed it over the hill toward the river, where it sat. Apparently, the truck was magnetic, because after that, that's where they threw all the mechanical junk, car parts and scrap steel, which eventually became a large pile. Later, my brother and I got the old truck running, which surprised and seemed to please our dad. We kept tinkering, and one day we decided we would weld a circular saw blade to the driveshaft of the truck and turn it into an unprotected saw mill. Dad stopped us and made us remove the blade, putting an end to our career as budding sawmill operators.

Perhaps all of these projects stopped substantially short of perfection, but each of them perpetuated our dream for the next step. Overall, we got pretty good at making things work, which I guess you could call junior inventing.

Because of our projects, our home became the gathering place for all the neighborhood children. Those children, from perhaps poorer homes, were in awe of all the "projects" in our backyard.

But not all neighborhood boys were invited. In fact, the Stevenson boys, Jack and Bill, were our committed enemies. Their home was just the right distance across the creek, as was their backyard for our giant "Howitzer" sling shot we'd built under our apple tree. Handy green apples were our ammunition. They easily bounced off their tin roofed home. Aiming it directly at Jack and Bill put them into hurried flight if they dared venture into sight. The Stevenson's pig lot was also conveniently nearby, and a resounding grunt could determine the accuracy of shots. But when apple season was over, we were at a disadvantage. The Stevenson boys were larger and they remembered our long-distance apple pelting.

Fishing & Hunting

The opportunities to explore shallow caves, build log cabins or just fool around—there was fun aplenty in the creeks, hills, and mountains surrounding our home. Elk River was at our back door—and sometimes in our basement—so swimming, fishing, and boating in it occupied our springs and summers.

When we didn't have a boat, we borrowed one from neighbors and we fished and ran trot lines across the river. We swam all summer, but we still helped Dad at the service station and Mother at the restaurant. Buddy Foglesong, my Aunt Anna's son-in-law, used to visit with his wife, Pauline, my first cousin. They would drive up from Charleston, where they lived, to our home in Clay and stay with us. I was happy when Dad said I could paddle Buddy around in my boat on the Elk River so he could go fishing.

He was a fly fisherman who I'd watch for hours as we talked. One Christmas, when I was probably about 13, Buddy gave me a fly rod and reel, and a set of 32 fishing flies. I was now in business as a fly fisherman! Fishing with the fly rod was not only momentous, but a hobby I'd happily pursue for the rest of my life.

The boat we had had been a "gift" from the river. It was a 16-foot poplar "jon boat" that was hand-made by someone. Flat-bottomed, jon boats are easy to paddle on calm water, which was perfect for our use on the Elk River. We first spotted the boat after the river had risen following a storm; it was jammed into a pile of debris.

It must have broken loose during the storm and floated down the river, coming to rest behind our house. Naaman Jr., and I swam out, got it loose and towed it home. We had a boat! We quickly used it to paddle around, explore and fish. Early on, we'd just cut a willow branch, attach a line, get some worms and we'd fish for hours. I caught bluegill, sunfish and bass. The family ate the fish I caught, with Mother frying them in a cornmeal batter. As I wasn't yet 18, I was too young to need a fishing license.

Hunting was made easy by the wooded nature of the hills around our home and our father's tolerance of our use of .22 rifles and .410 shotguns. The reality is that the squirrels, rabbits, and other animals were also tolerant of our weapons, because they could hear us coming from a mile away.

I used to go hunting, and I had a Winchester Model 69 single-shot .22 rifle that I earned by winning a state contest one summer when I was a boy. The contest was held in order to reduce the pressure on West Virginia fish, so the aim was to see who could kill the most water snakes and "water dogs" (North American river otters). My dog "Peanuts" and I went out every day, catching and killing water snakes and water dogs. I turned in the greatest number of snake heads and water dog heads from our area. I seem to remember I turned about 50 or so water dog heads and easily over 100 water snake heads, and I won the rifle and ten boxes of shells.

Dad had given me my first dog when I was about 4 or 5. He felt it important for us to understand responsibility and how to care for something other than yourself. He always said, "They only have what you hand them," which was a way of saying when you accept responsibility for an animal (or anything else), you accept the responsibility of its care.

The first dog I really remember was Peanuts. Peanuts was a black and brown Feist dog who assisted me in my many hunts for snakes and otters. Feist dogs are not a pure breed. They are a type of small hunting dog interbred to track and hunt above-ground prey.

Sadly, for me, Naaman Jr., bobbed Peanuts' tail. "All Feists have to have a short tail," he said. I didn't want him to do it and never liked it. (Traditionally, Feist dogs are felt to work prey better if their tail is bobbed. It has been a convention in rural areas for many decades.)

I had Peanuts for about five years until he simply disappeared one day. Living near a service station at a busy state highway intersection was very hazardous for animals. He was probably hit by a car and went off to die. I always hoped Peanuts would return some day, but he didn't.

Young "Moonshiners"

The Stevenson family lived next door to us. One day, we overheard our fathers talking about making "moonshine." But since no one had a still, it was really only beer or wine they were discussing. Mr. Scott Stevenson, his boys and my dad were making it in the basement of the Stevenson's house, and Naaman Jr., and I decided to join them in their enterprise by making some of our own.

We knew you had to have yeast, so we "borrowed" some along with Mother's fruit jars and sugar. We had all the water we needed.

In a few days, my friends Jack and Arthur Stevenson, two of Mr. Stevenson's sons, said their father accused some people of coming in and "stealing his yeast" to make moonshine. (Well, it was us, Jack, Arthur, Naaman Jr., and myself. Mr. Stevenson was the un-witting supplier of the yeast we had "borrowed.")

We mixed the ingredients and divided the mixture in our Mother's canning jars. We knew it had to "set" for a few days in a cool area to start the process. We thought the creek was the best place for us to hide our experiment. But some boys from up the creek who were wading in our area looking for "crawadadllers" (crayfish), discovered our jars and took them.

As for the actual illicit drink, the neighborhood men and our Dad made it together, fermenting it in the Stevenson's cellar.

WINSTON SHELTON, CRIME SCENE PHOTOGRAPHER

I came into owning a camera this way: a kid in high school had an ancient relative who passed away and had a 5 x 7 view camera. I think I gave him $15 or $20 and got a whole outfit: camera, tripod, everything. I became a photographer for the football team.

Having a camera opened up an entirely new world of experiences for me. The restaurant stayed open all night, so there were police constantly at the restaurant, and we became friends with them. They asked me if I'd photograph accident or crime scenes for them, and I said of course. I was always accessible to them: If I was in

THURSDAY, APRIL 4, 1940.

MYSTERY AUTO BLAST KILLS WEST VIRGINIAN

Coal Firm Head Blown To Bits While In Car

By The Associated Press.

CLAY, W. Va., April 4—J. V. Hinshelwood, 49-year-old coal company superintendent, was killed Wednesday by an explosion in his automobile while driving from Dundon to Widen in Clay county.

Reports were that Hinshelwood, general superintendent of the Elk River Coal & Lumber Co.'s operation since 1927, was alone in the car at the time of the blast. His body was badly mutilated.

The Elk river operation at Widen is one of the few non-union operations in West Virginia. A case is pending before the national labor relations board in which the United Mine Workers claim to represent a majority of the 700 workers, while an independent employes' association has intervened on the ground it represents a majority.

Mrs. Maxine Mullins, who visited the scene soon after the explosion was reported, described the results as "the most horrible thing I have ever seen."

Hinshelwood was a member of the Clay county school board.

INVESTIGATORS BEGIN

school, they'd pick me up and take me to a crime scene and I'd photograph it. It was mostly accidents I was photographing, but there was one crime scene that included a Mr. (J. Valentine) Hinshelwood, who was a general superintendent of the Elk River Coal and Lumber Co. mines. It was a non-union mining operation in Widen, West Virginia, which was nearby us.

That morning, I was working at the service station with Tony, my brother-in-law. He said he had to take some gas to Mr. Hinshelwood, who'd run out of gas about five miles from us. I joined him, and we got into the truck and drove until we found Mr. Hinshelwood and his Ford Coupe. Tony filled his tank and told him to start the car, but it didn't start. Tony raised the hood, replaced a distributor wire and said, "Now try it," and the vehicle ran. Tony put the hood down and off we went. It was in the morning, maybe 10 o'clock.

Once we returned, I went down to the high school to play basketball, just a pick-up game. But sometime after, the police came in the gym to get me. They asked me if I'd like to take pictures of Mr. Hinshelwood, who'd been killed when his car had been blown up at Widen Ridge. So, I went along with them.

I recall that it must have been fall because the woods were on fire from where the explosion had spread. I guess it had happened a couple of hours prior to our arrival.

They took me inside the roped-off perimeter, and there was Hinshelwood in the driver's seat. He was without arms or legs, his innards were out, but amazingly his chest and head were largely intact. I photographed him and the vehicle, and I then helped them search the scene for clues to what happened. As I was looking around I noticed something unusual among the leaves. I bent down to brush the leaves away and saw what it was: a shoe, a sock and a couple of leg bones, up to about mid-calf, sticking out.

NO CLUES FOUND IN HINSHELWOOD CASE; FUNERAL IS TODAY

Clay, W. Va., April 5. (U.P)—State police and Clay county authorities had "nothing to report" today in their investigation of the explosion which killed J. V. R. Hinshelwood, 49, coal company executive.

Superintendent Charles C. Tallman of the state police said, however, it had been determined that "high explosive, the exact nature of which is uncertain," caused the blast in which Hinshelwood was blown to bits and his automobile wrecked on Wednesday.

The Bureau of Criminal Identification at Charleston was examing the auto wreckage.

"The state police department will conduct a full investigation but has nothing to report at this time," Tallman said.

Private funeral services were to be conducted today at Charleston for Hinshelwood. At the same hour, employes of the Elk River Coal and Lumber Co. where Hinshelwood was superintendent, will hold memorial services in the Y.M.C.A. at Widen, W. Va., home of the firm.

Of course, I told the police about our helping Mr. Hinshelwood with his car earlier in the day, and so they were asking lots of questions.

From what I recall, they wondered if whatever they'd done to rig that car to explode was what made that distributor wire come loose. The police told me that normally that type of explosion happened when someone started the car, but that didn't happen to Hinshelwood. For whatever reason, it happened later. Everyone surmised it was likely the mine union that rigged the device. Everything that was adverse was done by the union in those days.

As you can imagine, we were surprised Tony didn't get killed, and that's what we reflected on that day.

Even though I was just 16 or 17 at the time, I wasn't horrified by what I saw that day. We lived in the mountains, and accidents were frequent because the roads could be treacherous. So, I'd been to a lot of accident scenes; we were steeled to automobile accidents.

One day near the service station, a terrible one happened. Had my back not been turned, I'd have seen it happen. Across the road there was a rock crusher set up by the state road commission. It was elevated off the road so you could back a truck up underneath it and move it. A car came past the station too fast and then started sliding. It hit the structure that was supporting the rock crusher, and the whole thing came on down on the two men in the car. We ran up there to see one man dead and the other dying.

After High School, Off to College

After finishing high school in 1939, I decided to stay out of school for a couple of years before starting to college to become an attorney. During that time, I worked for my father as a truck driver, a block setter on his sawmill and a caretaker of the mill's horses. I kept lanterns ready for lighting, drew water from a well to drink, stoked wood fires for stoves—for cooking and heat—kept the outhouses stocked with Sears Roebuck "wish books," you name it.

Winston Shelton, quarterback (No. 19) for the 1941 Glenville College Pioneers.

Attending Glenville College in 1941 may have been to satisfy my desire to play football as opposed to focusing on becoming an attorney. I was the only student on campus that owned a camera, so I was quickly chosen as the Staff Photographer of the college newspaper, the *Glenville Mercury*. In any event, both college and my becoming a lawyer were interrupted by World War II.

I joined the U.S. Army and had been ordered to appear at the barracks at the Fort Hayes Reception Center near Columbus, Ohio, on May 15, 1943.

Knowing I'd be issued a new uniform, I showed up in a green pajama shirt and trousers. I endured a battery of tests (some of which resulted in my later being selected for the Army Specialized Training program—more on that later), and enjoyed a very crude, very fast, short haircut.

I also remember an outstanding battery of injections, followed by immediate departure to Infantry Basic Training in Camp Fannin Texas, near Tyler. There, the injections continued weekly, and many men around me fell on their faces as they received the shots.

My company initially consisted of about 200 men, but after a few weeks, about 10 percent of them had "fallen out"—as in "on their faces," as early in the day as Reveille. Often it was so hot that men would fall over on their rifles, injuring themselves badly. Injections for smallpox soon followed.

The food was awful. The men complained about the coffee. When they couldn't drink all of it, the cooks would just keep the bad coffee and serve it later as "iced coffee." The cooks had been given incentives to save money, so they'd save money on their food budget by making awful food and drink. As a result, I dropped from 178 pounds to 168 very quickly.

Having survived Advanced Basic Training, I was slated to travel and join the 104th Infantry Division in New Jersey, a group destined to liberate Axis Occupied France. I was assigned to General Terry Allen's 104th Timberwolf Division, which had been shot up pretty bad in North Africa. But while my compatriot soldier friends were sent overseas, that wonderfully logical process that the Army uses to make its assignments decided that I should go to Princeton, New Jersey, instead to study engineering. Here's how that happened.

An Army-uniformed Private Winston Shelton at Princeton University, circa 1944.

I was fully outfitted, in uniform with my duffle bag and traveling on a troop train through the Northeast Corridor. All of a sudden, I heard a sergeant coming through the train calling for "Private Shelton," and 24 soldiers were trailing behind him. We were all put off the train at Princeton Junction, yet I didn't know what to think. We were told nothing. We left the train and were met by the Professor of Military Science and Tactics and told to await the train that would shuttle us to Princeton.

During our short wait, we were surprised to see Albert Einstein, dressed as always: suntan trousers and sweatshirt, and that unmistakable disarrayed gray hair. He also was waiting for the shuttle. Einstein lived at 112 Mercer Street in Princeton and used to enjoy sitting at the station and watching the trains go by. More than once he employed his experience of observing the trains there to explain the practical aspects of his General Theory of Relativity.

We arrived at Princeton University and were assigned to a master sergeant who took us to our quarters. He was the first military man I saw when we arrived on campus, and the last man I saw as I left that campus. He was our shepherd, but not a pleasant person to be with, offering no companionship at all. He was a completely indifferent person who had nothing to say about anything you might say to him. We soon learned to say nothing to him.

I was assigned to Holder Hall and told I would be attending the Engineering and Applied Science School. I used to credit my having been selected to one day back in basic training, when I was standing at attention during one of our scheduled Saturday inspections. I had perfected looking straight ahead while not looking at anything. An officer walked by, looked me over and said, "That's a fine position of a soldier, soldier." He asked an aide to note my name. I used to really think that was the start of the Army taking notice of me.

But the real reason was I had taken the Army General Classification Test and exceeded the minimum scores. I was never given a copy of my grades and I've never known how well I tested. But I quickly found myself in with a real bunch of geniuses at Princeton. I had been accepted into the Army Specialized Training Program (ASTP).

The Army Specialized Training Program

The ASTP was instituted by the United States Army during World War II to meet wartime demands both for junior officers and soldiers with technical skills. Conducted at multiple American universities, it offered training in such fields as engineering, foreign languages and medicine.

The program was approved in September 1942 and implemented in December that year. The entry requirements were very high: a minimum of 115 (later 120) on the Army OCT-X3 Examination for Officers Candidate School (a Stanford-Binet-type IQ test), compared to 110 for OCS candidates. All new soldiers who had been accepted into the ASTP were required to complete 13 weeks of infantry basic training before being assigned to a college campus. My basic training was at Camp Fannin in Tyler, Texas.

Col. Henry Beukema, a professor of history at West Point, was named director of the ASTP program. He was responsible for sending 200,000 soldiers to 227 colleges at a cost of $127 million. While high school graduates at least 17 years of age, but less than

Three Princeton University ASTP buddies, Private Vala-chovic, Private Stewart and Private Shelton, circa 1944.

18, were offered a chance to apply, the majority of participants were already on active duty in the Army.

The highly accelerated ASTP program was offered at 227 land-grant universities around the country. Students were expected to complete a four-year program in 18 months with a bachelor's degree and a military commission. A minimum of 25 class-time hours per quarter were required to meet the compressed schedule.

Intensive courses were offered in engineering, science, medicine, dentistry, personnel psychology, and different foreign languages. While in academic training, the soldiers were on active duty, in uniform, under military discipline, and received regular army pay. Recruits marched to class in groups, ate in mess halls located in the barracks, and trained in the fields around the campus. The soldiers' week featured 59 hours of "supervised activity," including at least 24 of classroom and lab work, 24 of required study, six of vigorous physical instruction, and five of military instruction.

At its height in December 1943, about 140,000 men were enrolled in the program. In January 1944, Col. Beukema reported to a U.S. Congressional investigating committee that ASTP was more demanding than either West Point or the Naval Academy.

I loved being at Princeton, I loved the campus. We did not mix in with the general student population beyond "eating clubs," which were primary residences and forerunners of sororities and fraternities. The normal Princeton life was, for the first-year students, living in a dormitory. When we were there, the military students occupied the standard dormitories, and the residential students occupied the eating clubs, which were located on Princeton Avenue. Occasionally, those students would invite us to come around to an eating club, and we got to know a few of them. I was even invited to a party one time, but they were not in our classes at all.

Life in the ASTP

Every day began with reveille played on a recorded bugle call. We would assemble in Holder Hall, which was notable for its Tudor exterior and spacious interior residences.

A tradition at Princeton was a to carve your name and personal mottoes, etc., into various surfaces with a knife. Tables, chairs, window sills—all were defaced by many varied and deep carvings. I don't recall carving my name into anything.

We dined in Henry Hall as freshman students, but when we became sophomores, we were allowed to dine in the eating clubs. The Howard Johnson restaurant chain provided catered meal services for many of the clubs.

We had a very rigorous educational program. The Army made a point of telling everyone we would earn a four-year degree in less than 18 months. A typical class day went like so:

After reveille, we were in class by 8 a.m. We had our lunch at noon and we were back in school at 1 p.m. Lecture labs followed at 3 p.m. followed by military training until 5 p.m. There was no study allowed in the late afternoon until the call of formal retreat, which was a dress-uniform flag ceremony. We were then allowed to have dinner and we had to be back in our rooms—quarters, as the military called them—at 7 p.m. That was our scheduled study time. Most in the program were very studious, but early on I said, "I'm not going to destroy my health staying up half the night studying," but I often did. (One reason to study is if you didn't pass, you were mustered out of the ASTP program and sent to the front lines, rejoining the 104th Timberwolves.)

The grading system was ranked from 1 through 7, with 1 being the highest grade. I never received a grade higher than a 3 or one lower than a 5. I felt my fellow students were all geniuses, every one of them, except for me. Some 1,200 ASTP students began the program at Princeton, and only 25 of us survived and became electrical engineering students. We all felt lucky to avoid being sent to the front.

A uniformed Winston Shelton.

Still, we were more than a bit puzzled about our little group, how we had been selected and why we were there. Thirteen in our group were Jewish and 12 were Gentiles. An odd coincidence was that we were all superior marksmen. Each of us had earned the highest marks as sharpshooters.

In our group were twin brothers, Aaron and Milton Fivush. Aaron made it all the way through the program, but Milton was one of those who flunked out. So, he was sent to the front. From the front, Milton invented a unique way to tell us where the 104th was stationed every time he sent Aaron a letter. In those days, military personnel could send a letter without postage by simply writing "APO, Service" (Army Post Office), and under that write one's Army serial number (a.k.a. service number) in the area on an envelope where you would normally affix a postage stamp. Instead of using his serial number, Milton used the longitude and latitude coordinates of his current location, stringing them together to look like a service number. Writing 50420621 on the envelope would get you very close to the real location of 50° 42' 31" N 06° 21' 46" E, a position on the Germany-Belgium border. Pretty creative.

Despite the grind, I did have some fun while at Princeton. I acquired a girlfriend while playing "speedball," a combination of handball and soccer, and an intramural sport. This particular girl had a boyfriend who was on the opposing team, playing goalie. While defending a shot from me, he somehow ended up with a double compound fracture of the leg. It was gruesome: both bones were sticking through the skin of his leg after our skirmish.

I got the girl.

When we were allowed to leave campus—very rare times when we had no assigned study or duties—we would often take a bus to Trenton, N.J., and go to movies and bars. We frequented a storied tavern, the Yankee Doodle Tap Room, in the restaurant located inside the Nassau Inn. The tavern had heavy oak tables and chairs literally covered in deeply carved names and slogans (that tradition again). The back wall of the Tap Room featured a huge mural of Yankee Doodle painted by Norman Rockwell. It's still there today.

Interestingly, the other students at Princeton paid no particular attention to us as we went about our time there. We were simply Army men in school, not combat. We didn't ask "Why?" nor did anyone else.

Doc Tolson, a Mentor

I met a man, William Arthur Tolson, and we became good friends. I was out one day in a borrowed canoe on an afternoon date with a girl at one of the few places during a day that afforded privacy. We were on Lake Carnegie, which had been formed by damming the Millstone River. There were a number of rivulets and small inlets on the edge of the lake. We pushed up into a rivulet and anchored the boat. I climbed out of the boat and was swinging on a branch over the lake to impress the girl when a man came by and asked if we'd rather go to his house and have a beer. We said yes. He introduced himself as William Tolson.

"Doc" Tolson was a radio engineer with RCA. He'd had an impressive past, having started one of the first radio stations in America, WTAW (the last three call letters were his initials backwards) in Waco, Texas. He broadcast the first radio broadcast play-by-play coverage of a football game in history on November 24, 1921. The game, the Turkey Bowl between Texas A&M and the University of Texas, was broadcast using a unique code invented by Tolson, to send Morse code coverage of the plays to a remote announcer in Waco. A series of abbreviations were used to make the transmissions speedy. "T" represented Texas, "A," Aggies, "B," ball, "Y," yard line, "FP," forward pass, "G" for gain, and "L" for loss. Thus, "TB A 45Y" translated to "Texas ball on the Aggies' 45-yard line." Upon receiving the Morse code play-by-play information, the announcer was able to relate the game in almost real time—a story that fascinated me! Doc Tolson later became part of the huge RCA Research Laboratories in Camden, New Jersey. Since my studies already were in communications and electrical engineering, we became friends. Despite his accomplishments, he was a very down-to-earth person. He and his wife had a nice home in Princeton, but they chose to live in that camp near the water, so I'd visit them by canoe since I had no car. Socializing with him was a wonderful education that I was very fortunate to receive.

The Army had decided I was to become a communications electrical engineer. Finishing the curriculum at Princeton, I was assigned to the Army Signal Corps engineering laboratories at Fort Monmouth, New Jersey, along with the other 24 graduates.

There, we participated in various radar and communications projects as technicians and in the testing of advanced communication relay station equipment known as AN/TRC5 and AN/TRC6, the Army Navy Transportable Radio Communications 5 series (created by RCA) and the 6 series (created by Bell Laboratories). The equipment operated at much higher frequencies than then-current standards of 70 to 100 mega-cycles. The new AN/TRC radio relay stations used neither FM nor AM radio waves. It instead employed one signal in the microwave region, SHF (Super High Frequency) and then chopped that signal into eight pieces, providing eight channels simultaneously. That was twice the capacity of the old TRC-1 equipment. The system could provide reliable radio relay service during battle over a distance of 600 miles, and it was referred to in the military as a "long-haul" microwave radio relay system.

The Army Navy Transportable Radio Communications unit in the field during operational testing.

Since these tests occurred in San Francisco, our group was relocated there. The tests involved line-of-sight relay links from our location at the Presidio (then a military base) to Los Angeles. We had three crews to man the terminals and links from the Presidio to the Los Angeles Signal Depot, with relays at Mt. Hamilton, Catalina Island and many other locations.

We first took a six-week training program, learning all the technical details. That made us field engineers on both the 5 and the 6 series of relay stations. There were eight field engineers at each station to set up and maintain communications. The tests of the AN/TRC6, followed by the AN/TRC5, were continuous for about three months. We would input at one end, *"The quick brown fox jumped over the lazy dog,"* and we would record the message at the other end. With eight channels and carriers on each channel, we had 32 simultaneous messaging opportunities.

I loved living in San Francisco as there was so much to do there! Though I did have an interesting and curious interaction with my landlord, one Ms. Lusk. I don't know that I'd call it a conflict or dispute, but I had some concerns with my rent. As I was moving into the upstairs of her place, some other military men were moving out, and they told me the $55 rent she was charging was above the government-approved ($35) rent for soldiers. So that bothered me, of course, but I didn't immediately know how to address that.

Before long, I discovered she played her radio quite loudly, for she was hard of hearing, and that radio was playing in her living room, right below my room. That gave me an idea … .

I effectively jammed her radio so she couldn't listen to the programs she was tuning in to. Using a device I'd used in the military, I could produce an intermediate frequency that would make extra sounds on her radio—things like a series of boom-boom-booms or a long, loud squeak. Somehow, she'd learned I was involved in radio work for the military, and she asked if I could fix it, and I did. Twice. Of course, I didn't charge her cash to do it. I got free rent for a couple of months.

Late in the Fort Monmouth laboratories assignment, we were gathered together by a young lieutenant whom we did not know. He told us we were going to Eniwetok (also known as Bikini Atoll), a tiny island in the Southeast Pacific Ocean, to witness an atomic bomb test. Truthfully, I wasn't all that interested in going, and by this point in my military career, the war had ended, and we were simply waiting to get enough points to be discharged. Most interestingly, we also were told that our efforts as engineering technicians while at Princeton, were applied to the Manhattan Project, the highly secret effort to create the first atomic bombs used on the Japanese cities of Hiroshima and Nagasaki. Even though we'd remain unneeded until the atomic bomb testing at Bikini Atoll, I opted instead to leave the Army in 1945. Some might not believe this (or understand it), but I regretted not going to the front during the war. When you've been in the presence of men who've been there and been shot at and shot up, you get quite a conscience about not being there and fighting alongside them and doing your duty, too.

BACK TO COLLEGE

I left the Army to continue my education in engineering at Glenville State College in West Virginia. During my two years there prior to my Army enlistment, I had failed to letter in varsity football. So, in the fall of 1945, I succeeded in lettering as a starting guard on that team.

Then for that year's second semester, I enrolled at West Virginia University. I found out what everyone learns when they attempt to change schools at the college level: registrars simply don't believe you've taken a required course until you've taken *their* required course. I therefore found myself repeating much of the work already completed at Princeton University and experienced in the Army Specialized Training Program.

Weathering that backslide, I became a West Virginia University electrical engineer and received my BSEE degree in May of 1948.

Winston The Pugilist

I first got interested in boxing some time around 1935, after I'd been in a few fights—scraps, really—and I found I kind of liked it. I dabbled a bit in boxing again when I was at Princeton with the Army Specialized Training Program, and I fought three or four times in the 18 months I was there. But I did most of my boxing when I was at Fort Monmouth, New Jersey. I was part of the Army Signal Corps and stationed there from 1944 through late '45.

Boxing provided me some year-round athleticism, and it kept me out of other military activities I wanted to avoid anyway, things like drills. I went out for the Company A boxing team, for which I fought every month I was there. I weighed 168 pounds, which made me a middleweight then, and I won 18 out of my 21 bouts. I was pretty good at it.

Sure, it could get pretty rough, but I think I largely liked it because I did most of the beating up instead of getting beaten up! As I mentioned, I really liked the athleticism, and it was a good sport for a football player, particularly a lineman; they have to play with their hands closed. You could really use them effectively when you understood how to use them kind of like a boxer. If you've boxed,

Athletics were a part of Winston's life during college.

people didn't like to play football against you.

Our boxing was taken quite seriously. Men would come from New York, Madison Square Garden specifically, to watch us box. They were looking for people they might someday bring to Madison Square Garden to box in a Friday or Saturday night match. Sometimes they'd bring in professionals for us to box. They were tough, some really rough characters. The trainers who typically came out of Madison Square Garden to work with us fostered some real roughness and crudeness among the boxers. I don't recall anything that was commendable about any of them.

I'm pretty certain that a man named Ruby Goldstein was among them, and I liked him. He was a boxer at some point in his life, but he was a referee at Madison Square Garden when I met him. I think he was a friend of the company commander, or maybe a friend of the man in charge of our boxing team, so he took an interest in us. Once, when he was showing me a move, he became fascinated with this shuffle I did. So, he told me to try it on him, and as

I came in to parry one hand at him, he made this quick move and boxed both my jaws—at the same time! He knew what I was going to do and what he was going to do in response, and he delivered it perfectly. I loved that about boxing, the thought and self-control associated with it.

When I fought, what worked well for me was to go through the first three or four rounds and endure some substantial exchanges in order to get a guy sized up. Then, I'd come out of my corner, shuffle across the floor really fast toward where he was standing and, with a left hook, put him on the floor.

I believe I was probably a better athlete than most of those guys because they were boxers only, and not athletes with a lot of stamina. But I can tell you, many times when I'd gotten out of those matches and was headed to the locker room, I'd pass the shower, lie down on a bench, pull a wastebasket over, and I'd stick my head over it and vomit into it. Even a short boxing match is so intense.

I took some beatings, too. Once, I'd stayed in the corner too long as this guy was working on me, and as I tried to come out of there, the guy hit me on the point of the chin, and my head snapped back and hit the post. It was a serious head injury, which later gave me seizures. Luckily, after five or six of them, they went away.

One of the challenges of fighting at an Army base was you had so many people being shipped into and out of there, so often you'd not know who you were boxing next. Sometimes you got to see the other guy in action before you boxed him, but not always, and that made it difficult to know what to expect. Even if you knew how your opponent would fight, it still didn't mean you knew everything. In one fight, I had a man in front of me who I thought was not capable of an uppercut because he was so tall. So, I came in awfully low with my head down and he hit me with an uppercut that lifted me off the ground. Oh, he hit me hard! I went down, but I got back up. I don't recall whether he beat me or it was a draw, but what I remember is it made me mad that I underestimated him. I'd seen him box before and had a whole strategy for getting underneath him because of his height. But man, I didn't expect that!

I can't say that it was real Golden Gloves (sanctioned) boxing, but every time you won a match, you won a golden glove citation. Perhaps you accumulated points for your wins, though I don't recall exactly. But since I won 18 out of 21 fights, I'm sure I would have been the Fort Monmouth middleweight champ if I'd have stuck with it.

I quit boxing when I learned my company commander was betting on me to lose. That really offended me, the fact that he didn't care if his soldiers won, but instead whether he won money on our fights. The truth is he was a real asshole of a man, a guy who wore jodhpurs and always had a riding crop. Sometime after I quit the team, I learned that his wife shot him after she came home one day and determined he was in bed with the housekeeper. It's too bad that it didn't kill him. That was the kind of man we were dealing with—men, actually. The Army was full of such types.

A New Engineer at General Electric

Now 26 years old, I was recruited in 1948 by the General Electric Co. and assigned to its Home Laundry Department of the Major Appliance Division, located in Bridgeport, Connecticut. After a couple of weeks in the wringer engineering section, I was reassigned to the automatic washer plant at Trenton, New Jersey, where I was to work for the next four years.

I was hired in as a test engineer, which meant I was placed in a system that would keep you moving through departments for two years, with the expectation that during that time, a department would find you valuable and hire you as an employee for that department. The reality is that they saw such genius in me that they hired me right away.

No, really, I was hired in this way: During my first three months, I was assigned to the Testing Laboratory, where I tested the current G.E. automatic washing machine, known internally as model 1AW6B1. This was some washing machine! It had been designed principally by Thomas Theodore "Ted" Woodson. He had worked on the washing machine for G.E. during the war and the four years' time he spent on the project allowed him to greatly over-engineer the unit.

It was expensive as well, costing $349.75—equivalent to $3,500 in 2017 dollars. The unit was simultaneously overly complex and overly simple in many aspects of its design.

The unit had two water pumps, four knobs, two controllers and five electric motors inside!

The 1947 GE product introduction of the AW-6 automatic washer.

In typical G.E. fashion, existing parts were used rather than newly fabricated ones that might have done the job better. Some of the motors were simply repurposed oscillating fan motors that were very small and underpowered for the task of agitating a load of wet clothing. Lacking the torque necessary for quick, clean starts, I was tasked with troubleshooting that problem and many others. For example: customers reported that when they returned from an extended trip or a vacation, the machine leaked water when restarted. I determined the pump motors' seals would stick after the washing machine hadn't been used for a while, and when the under-powered motor was started, the seal would tear and allow water to leak.

I wanted to research the problem in every direction I could think of because I had been told my tenure was only a 90-day test. I didn't want to be let go at the end of three months because of a lack of having tried.

So, again in typical G.E. fashion, we immediately launched into tests with different seal faces on the pump housing. I backed up and instead wondered why the seals were sticking in the first place, so I decided to learn more about why things stick.

I called the Permatex Company, a firm with a long history in automotive sealants and lubricants, and visited their laboratory in Brooklyn, New York, to ask in person, "What makes things stick?" I learned a great deal more about the problems we were having with the pump motor seals.

In the end, Bill Dabrowski from the G.E. model shop helped me solve the problem. He machined a circular groove into the pump seal, we filled it with a waterproof automobile grease and the pump motor no longer leaked.

So I had passed the three-month test and promptly found myself placed in the Design Office of the Production Engineering Office on a new assignment. I was now to directly address ongoing engineering problems with automatic washers in current production.

I started in on the suspension of the washing machine, which had a unique set of three sprung suspension arms with dampers that allowed the wash tub (which was very heavy when full of water) to gyrate and flex inside the cabinet as the motor spun during the drain cycle. The bottom of the tub had three welded splines that were hung from springs on their corresponding dampers. When the unit was tilted on its side during shipment, installation or service, the tub assembly could slide out of the dampers and the unit wouldn't work.

I made an observation to my supervisor, Dick Gabriel, that the springs were located in the wrong position, and suggested the design would be better if the arrangement was turned upside down so the tub assembly couldn't drop down and out. When Dick said that wouldn't work, his supervisor said, "Wait a minute, I think that's a good idea," and he had us try my suggestion. Dick resented my having prevailed a little, but those things happened all the time in the Engineering department.

I was soon sent to Advanced Engineering, leaving the Production Engineering Office behind. There, I was put on a special team given the task of completely redesigning the corporation's flagship automatic washing machine. There I was again, working on the two-pump, two-controller, five-motor "wonder"!

Very slow sales of the unit saw its production dramatically lowered from 3,000 units per week to just 500 units per week. G.E. had a significant problem with this expensive, complex washing machine, and customers knew, as we did, that there were many, many fundamental problems. One example was the spin cycle's 1,140 RPM speed—extremely fast for such a heavy unit. When spinning the clothes, the entire unit literally danced across the floor. So, fellow engineers Ed Lipinski, Nick Detoro, myself and many others set to work on the unit.

First, we eliminated all the high-end features, cut the electric motor count down to two, and used just one pump to both fill the tub with water and discharge it. The company reconfigured the model number series to reflect our success, changing it from the "1A6" to the "1A5." The change indicated the reduced complexity of the washer line. It was one of the few times that a new G.E. model had a lower number than its predecessor. Not surprisingly, the revised model started selling well.

The cover of the owner's manual for Winston's re-designed 1948 GE AW-5 automatic washer. Look closely - two less knobs!

I also came up with a solution to a perpetual problem of clothes washers in that day: lost socks. Of course, they weren't truly lost, rather the agitator and the spinning of the machine could literally fling them outside the wash tub and into a water discharge tube. The problem was made worse when a sock wound up so far down that tube that it got into the water pump. To me, the solution was simple: add a single cross-hatched deflector at the opening of the discharge tube to catch any object that got down there. It wasn't a fine filter, like you'd use to filter coffee because the water would still need to flow back to the pump easily. It was one of those fixes that I was amazed no one else had considered.

In 1955, we started to address the need for better controls for the automatic washing machine. I took a Telechron clock motor (invented circa 1918 by Telechron, a G.E. subsidiary) and built a geared, cam timing control mechanism around it. I called it a "Face Cam Control," but the attorneys and the United States Patent

Trademark Office (USPTO) ended up calling it a "Timing Mechanism for Conducting a Selected One of a Plurality of Sequences of Operation." That mechanism is still used today on many, many appliances, and I'm proud to say that its patent bears my name.

In 1956, I had become a development engineer in the automatic washer section of the Home Laundry Department. I was given the project of researching the agitator and its motion during clothes washing to better understand how the process worked and how we could improve on it. In 18 months, the project was completed, and the results identified that it was "... mechanical work done by the agitator upon the clothes" in the water-detergency medium that separated the soil from the fabric; and the physics of detergency that "...maintained that separation as the medium and clothes were separated."

In layman's terms, we learned that inside the washtub of water, the agitator's action lifted the dirt away from the wet fabrics while the suspended detergent surrounded the lifted dirt particles and kept them away from the fabrics while the dirty wash water was spun out of the clothes and rinsed clean. A later and highly important document, identified in G.E. as TIS-56HL, documented our findings.

Following that research project, I developed a new spiral agitator post that was to be used on G.E. washing machines for years to come. In all, I worked in the Home Laundry Department for 15 years, but from time to time, I moved to projects outside that realm.

Around 1950, I was working on magnetic door gaskets for G.E. refrigerators. We were putting firecracker-sized magnets inside the door gaskets to make a tight seal when the door was closed. If a magnet was bad when those were installed in the door gasket assembly, the door wouldn't seal correctly, causing a rework on the line or a call back to the consumer's home.

Nick Detoro theorized that if the magnet was well magnetized, when dropped down a copper tube, it would slide down the tube more slowly than a poorly magnetized magnet. He knew that a good magnet developed a slight voltage as it descended, providing a counterforce that slowed it down. To test it, he inclined the copper tube, dropped in magnets good and bad, and the good magnet slid down the tube more slowly. A bad magnet just slid straight out.

For this simple and elegant insight, Nick won the G.E. "Charles Coffin Award," an honor named after the cofounder and first president of General Electric.

Dolly's World

Engineering always fascinated Winston Shelton, but he was captivated by Hazel Winifred "Dolly" Crider the moment he met her in 1948 at an Arthur Murray Dance Studio in Trenton, New Jersey.

"It was clear to me that she was a person of some substance—not to mention possessing all the equipment of a beautiful female," he recalls, smiling broadly. "Our first date was a trip to the Jersey shore for swimming. We had a great time on the beach."

Winston and four G.E. colleagues shared a five-room apartment that, understandably, was the common weekend party spot. Bubbly, bright and engaging, Dolly fit right in with the group, and became Winston's constant companion.

"She was the happiest person at a party you could ever imagine, and the most fun to be with," Winston recalls. "She was full of excitement and stories—clean stories, always."

While attending Rider University in nearby Lawrenceville, New Jersey, Dolly lived with and cared for her father, an affable widower with the impressive name "Sylvan Stearn Crider"—better known to the family as "Pop." Knowing that Winston played chess, Dolly said her father also was an avid player, and she set up a meeting between the two men.

"She fixed dinner for Pop, herself and me, and we played chess— while she fumed," he laughs. "He was a really good player, so I suppose we weren't showing her much attention."

As their courtship continued, marriage was discussed, but without a firm date. G.E. had plans to send Winston to Louisville, Ky., where it was building a new factory, and Dolly allowed that she'd like to join him there—though only after a last hurrah with her girlfriends. Eager to see Florida, New Orleans and Dallas, she planned the trip and even asked Winston to stay with and care for her father while she was gone. He agreed, and Dolly headed south.

"She was having the time of her life, and I called her up and tried

Winston and Dolly wed September 6, 1952.

to join her in New Orleans," Winston begins. Laughing, he adds, "But she said, 'No, not yet.' She pretty much said she didn't want me down there with her. Whatever they were doing must have been fun."

After a short stay in Dallas, she phoned Winston to tell him she'd had her fill and wanted to return to Trenton. He picked her up and brought her back to New Jersey, where they married on Sept. 6, 1952. They moved to Louisville that same year, to an apartment not far from G.E.'s temporary downtown offices. There, he and Dolly lived for three months while the first of Appliance Park's massive buildings was constructed. With Pop wintering in Florida with friends, Dolly and Winston began a search for property on which they could build their own house. Though having little savings of their own, the couple was motivated, Winston says, by a strong dislike of paying rent. Dolly's distaste for it outmatched even his, he says.

"When we moved to Louisville in 1952, we got an apartment at 3217 Utah St. We were paying $57.50 a month, but we just didn't like renting. We wanted to put our money toward a home for us. We talked about it quite a bit, and when I mentioned that we'd be living pretty lean in order to move out, Dolly said, "Well, at least we'd save $57.50 a month." Dolly wanted to be out here as much as I. She saw it as just another adventure. She saw so much of life in just that way.

"We were very serious about making money, which also meant that we designed our lives around some lean days," Winston recalls. "There weren't any expensive vacations or new cars early on because we didn't consider having those as the right thing to do. Dolly never considered any of it a sacrifice. It was sport for her."

Winston dug and built an outhouse, rigged a pump to bring creek water to the house, and spent much of his spare time cutting wood for the fireplace. Valerie, the first of their three children was added to the tiny abode in 1954.

Like her mother, Valerie Shelton loved the rustic setting that included Winston's favorite dog, Mink, and a cow named Bossie, who calved another named Snow. The family got around the property in their 1946 Willy's Jeep.

Dolly, Valerie says, was both smart and frugal enough to stretch Winston' $280 monthly salary to cover a list of expenses totaling just $180 a month.

The 3-acre lake was designed as a source of relaxation for Winston, but it became a source of fish and "frog legs so fresh, they jumped out of the pan! And I'm not kidding," Valerie says. Bordered by thick woodlands, the lake also attracted ducks, geese and peacocks, whose eggs often wound up on the Shelton table.

GrandPop Crider (Dolly's father) frequently put out trotlines attached to gallon milk jugs and baited with chicken necks to catch turtles in the lake for turtle soup. Seeing a milk jug move rapidly across the lake was always a source of excitement for the family. Pop would climb in the row boat and haul the turtles into the boat. The turtles would meet their maker on a stump in the front yard. Nests on the bank of the lake were also a source of duck eggs early in the spring that generally ended up on the family table.

That visiting friends were sometimes shocked to find the Sheltons living so humbly, Winston says, "None of that mattered to Dolly.

GrandPop Crider with the front yard stump chopping block.

She was living on her terms, and we were very happy there."

After a few years, Naaman Sr., and Opal moved to the home site, towing a mobile sawmill from West Virginia. Soon, Winston, his father and Naaman Jr., were felling timber on the property and sawing it into boards for Winston's family's home.

Amid the new construction, Dolly gave birth to daughter, Laura in 1957, and son, David in 1960. Compared to their first home, the structure was roomy for the five-member clan, and made comfortable with indoor plumbing and mechanical heat. But by Winston's own admission, the site was in a perpetual state of construction, which could irritate his wife.

As Winston left G.E. to form his own firm, his workload increased dramatically. Yet Valerie recalls it not derailing Dolly's life at all. Her mother loved her father, but Dolly was her own person.

"She filled her life with other things than just us, and I think she usually had a good time," she says.

She believes her mother's strong-willed nature was good for her dad in many ways. Winston not only admired Dolly's insistence on thinking for herself, her ability to do so kept his own singlemindedness in check.

"I think she was one of the few people who could stand up to him and make him see things another way than his," Valerie says. Smiling, she adds, "She ruled the roost, and he primarily did whatever she told him to do."

Though Dolly's life was full in every respect, Winston says it amazed him to witness her devotion to others. When he wanted to leave G.E., she insisted on earning a teaching degree to ensure the family had income while the business got off the ground.

"It was critical to her that we be taken care of, that her children be taken care of," he recalls, "I was infinitely proud that she would do that to help, and it was a big help."

In addition to her constant care for Pop Crider, Winston says she "loved my mother and father dearly. She made those two people feel like royalty… I realized I had a companion who would contribute to my career by being herself and taking care of others."

And sometimes by backing them off. Winston says Dolly wasn't afraid of confrontation if she felt someone had been wronged or disrespected. When a local police officer cited their son for speeding, Dolly so strongly believed David hadn't erred that she went to the police station and confronted the man.

"She found him and gave him a good lecture!" Winston says, grinning. Later, when details of the story emerged, it was clear the officer was in the right. When Winston visited the officer and apologized for Dolly's actions, the officer admitted he struggled to keep from laughing during the undue upbraiding. "She could be inclined to anger, especially in matters that involved her children… but as quick as she was to anger, she was just as quick to love."

Even when Winston annoyed her, as Valerie recalls. One morning she "awoke to a ruckus outside" and went to her bedroom window to see what was hap-

Dolly with David, Laura and Valerie and her favorite car - a mint green 1959 Cadillac Coupe DeVille.

pening. From her vantage point, she glimpsed Winston crouched beside his car, rising and ducking while Dolly lobbed eggs at him.

"Mother was throwing eggs at the top of the car, and Winston was ducking down to not get hit," she recalls. Curiously, he was grinning and chuckling. "I could hear him saying, 'Are you sure I can't bring you anything from the store? Milk?' An egg would splat on the car, and he'd duck. Then he'd pop up and say, 'Bread?' Splat, another egg! Eventually she stopped and I saw him snicker and drive off."

Winston smiles at the recollection, saying, "I know I'd done something wrong," but allows the root of the disagreement is now vague. "It might have been … well … I know I was constantly telling

Dolly that she was beautiful, even before she put her hair up or got made up for the day. She was, of course, flattered by it, but also a little incensed by it too because I'd flatter her about the same level when she was indeed beautiful and made up. So, I think that's what had pissed her off."

According to Winston, Dolly's combined high intellect and occasionally fiery nature combined to make her a formidable force in table games. Valerie says Dolly liked "nothing better than to drop the queen of spades on Winston in a game of hearts," but continually losing to Winston at chess motivated Dolly to master the game clandestinely.

"There came a point in our marriage when she started beating me at chess, and I got suspicious," Winston says. "All of a sudden, I find that I'm losing to her, and I'm thinking, 'What am I doing wrong?' When she started making moves I wasn't expecting, I asked her, 'Did you make two moves?' and she'd say, 'No, I didn't make two moves.'"

It turned out that Dolly had a secret. On Wednesdays, she'd leave the house, meeting the Douglass Chess Club in Louisville in order to improve her game. Valerie says the kids knew about it, "But we were sworn to secrecy." Winston knew she was leaving the house regularly on Wednesdays, but Dolly wouldn't reveal where.

"They were both such keen intellects and consequently competitive - all while being so in love. I honestly think he'd rather she was having an affair than brushing up on chess in order to beat him," Valerie says.

The truth came out when the couple went out to dinner. As they entered the restaurant and moved toward their table, Winston noticed Dolly exchanging knowing glances with chess club members Mr. and Mrs. Hugo Eberlein at a nearby table. Seeing the jig was up, she took Winston to the Eberlein's table. Mr. Eberlein said nonchalantly. "Haven't seen you at the chess club lately."

"It was then I learned they were teaching her," he says, smiling. "But I also discovered later that she had a whole stash of books on chess behind her side of the bed. And I think those books helped teach her some of the tricks she was now using on me."

Though Dolly never worked for Winston Industries, she traveled occasionally with Winston to tradeshows. There, she organized shopping excursions for other wives whose idea of a good time wasn't working an exhibit hall booth and selling restaurant supplies.

"We would go to Chicago for the National Restaurant Association Show together," Winston says. "She actually was in the booth with me some of the days, which gave us a social connection that was awfully nice.

"She'd take those ladies and go shopping, and I sometimes had trouble getting her home because she'd have so many appointments with the other ladies."

In 1990, however, Dolly's colorful life took a turn when she was stricken with liver damage caused by a then-unspecified disease. Years later, when diagnosed with Hepatitis C, doctors determined her hopes depended on a liver transplant and the wait for a donor organ began. According to daughter Laura Shelton, Dolly received a transplant on June 19, 1995, yet following the surgery, she remained unconscious until July 4. Her hospital stay lasted more than two months and was followed by weeks in a rehabilitation facility where she gained the strength to walk again. At home, she cared for herself and cooked occasional meals. But in the fall of 1996, when five malignant tumors were discovered on her transplanted liver, she was given a grim prognosis of two to three months to live.

Laura recalls Dolly's decline including occasional hallucinations in which she imagined Valerie having "a hole in her liver," though Laura determined she was recalling her own biopsy. When she convinced her mother Valerie didn't have cancer, she was relieved, as any mother would be.

As Dolly's health declined, home-health nurses were sent to care for her, and Winston slashed his work schedule to be by her side. Ever the learner, Winston asked the nurses to teach him the basics of giving shots and taking blood samples. He bathed her, read stories and poetry to her, yet the two longtime chess players didn't square off over the checkered board.

"You know, I don't know why we didn't, but the thought didn't occur to either of us," he says. Pausing to return in his mind to that time, he affirms with a smile and a shake of his head, "No, no chess."

With help from his children, Winston cared for her, working as little as an hour a day at the factory, only to ensure vital matters were addressed.

"I didn't want to surrender any responsibility for her care, and I didn't," he says. "That the family was close by was a great comfort to both of us. It was a year of devotion and the most comforting experience to be with her in that period of my life."

During Dolly's illness, David was appointed CEO of Winston Industries in 1996, holding that position until 2010.

On February 13, 1997, Dolly passed away. Winston's wife, best friend, confidant and friendly competitor was gone at age 69. Near her bed, a silver, heart-shaped balloon from Winston, wishing her a happy Valentine's Day, remained tethered to a TV cabinet for weeks.

When a crowd gathered for Dolly's funeral, the mood was expectedly somber. Winston, however, sought to deliver an uplifting message to her many grieving relatives and friends.

"We weren't particularly religious, so I conducted her funeral," Winston recalls. "And as I looked at my grandchildren, who were crying, I said, 'I've never seen a room where Dolly created unhappiness, and this shouldn't be one either. She had a glorious life, and I hope you could appreciate that, not in sadness, but in merriment.'"

Yet eventually he, too, succumbed to melancholia, wondering at age 75 what to do next now that a year spent beside his sick wife had ended.

"When you give all you've got to a person in that situation, you don't have anything else to give after that," he says. "Her absence was a vacuum, and for a long while, nothing seemed worthwhile or important."

Not surprisingly, the siren song of work drew him back to the factory with renewed energy for his company. A year largely spent away from Winston Industries provided him a new perspective about his career, and at 75 years old, he dove back in.

"The business called my attention back to it, and I was eager to attend to it," he says. "Sometimes, when dedicating your life to another, that unique inspiration gets you out of yourself and gets you thinking about really important matters… I enjoyed coming back."

End note: Sometime after Dolly's passing, Winston and Joyce Daniels, a longtime friend who'd also lost her spouse, sought to share their grief and encourage each other in coping with their losses. According to Winston, their meetings revealed the pair had many things in common, including a love of fishing.

Little time passed before the two began discussing a future together, and marriage followed in 1999. With daily assistance, Winston still lives at home, while Joyce currently lives in an elder-care facility. In 2017, the two celebrated their 18th wedding anniversary.

To G.E.'s Appliance Park in Louisville, Kentucky

In 1952, I was assigned to work at G.E.'s brand new Appliance Park in Louisville. Covering 1,000 acres in the city's suburbs, the factory would eventually employ 25,000 workers at its peak. It was an exciting opportunity to move there and continue working in the Home Laundry Division.

But as excited as I was about the relocation—the move was a start to a new life for my wife and me—I acknowledged some growing discomfort within: that of my relationship with my supervisors at G.E. As much as my work at G.E. taught and inspired me, as early as my time at the Trenton plant, I was becoming frustrated with the corporation's reluctance to easily accept innovation—even when it was obvious the suggested changes were vast improvements over old ways. When I offered ideas and dockets for improvement, there was all too much caution as to their acceptance—sometimes, even outright rejection of what clearly was an improved design.

It seemed there was, on the one hand, a spirit and demand for ideas, while, on the other hand, there were those who were cautious to a

Winston conferring with a fellow engineer in Appliance Park's Building 1. The building was large enough to "hold 10 football fields."

fault when new ideas were offered. At that point, as much respect as I had for G.E., I bore just as much disrespect.

Amid that frustration, there were some who were my champions. One supervisor, Harold "Socks" Stocking, saw something different in me and sponsored me for special engineering projects. Just his wonderful presence made a better engineer out of me, especially when he accused me of having more talent than I thought I had. He realized I could fix things because solutions to many problems were obvious to me, but not always to others.

Another helpful colleague was John Ryan, a very bright, very good engineer, though not intuitive in the same way I was. He saw something in me and brought me a book on Buckingham's pi theorem. He told me to read it, and let me tell you, it opened my mind—tremendously so! At that time, we had an automatic washer that washed just 8 pounds of clothes, and John believed it should wash more than 8 pounds. And after reading that book, I redesigned the washing system consistent with the teaching of Buckingham's pi theorem to wash 12 pounds using a bigger motor. Eventually, I got it to a point that it washed a 15-pound load all within its existing framework.

Still, my work met with frustration with increasing regularity. G.E. was highly political and more importantly social as regards the culture of drinking after work. Many of my colleagues would leave work early, head out to the cocktail lounge and get home late (which is how they transacted business), and the next day I might have some assignments as a result of that cocktail hour. I was never invited to those, was never asked to go, nor did I ask to go.

To find an audience for an idea I had, I took a small risk and entered a private dining room (for people who were my bosses back then) and took a seat. Sitting there was Jim Goss, the general manager of the Home Laundry Division, and John Ryan. In a note I'd written to John, I'd expressed to him that I found fault with the way G.E. recruited engineers. My contention was that they hired only good engineering students, rather than people with experience in practical application of that education.

I'd been with the company long enough to know that its best engineers were farm boys or, better put, problem solvers who'd worked around mechanical things. Growing up working at my father's sawmill, I had problems to solve every day, so at G.E., it was a natural

Winston (at left, wearing glasses) attending a birthday party at Appliance Park's Building 1.

thing for me to say, "Why don't you do this or try that?" I tended to think of a practical approach such as "sawmill engineering," and I believed the company should seek out people who'd had that kind of hands-on, mechanical experience before getting an engineering degree in college. I didn't meet with much agreement on the issue.

So many of the people G.E. hired were Tau Beta Pi members (a revered national engineering society), graduate-level people and a totally different class of people from me. They simply wouldn't listen, and it was a universal, never-ending problem. When I began to realize that the people who were reviewing my ideas for change were the same people who had had the opportunity to develop those ideas a few months prior, I sensed they were embarrassed by my obvious solutions. I just lived and thought simpler than most. John Ryan, who was my biggest champion, looked at problems like a theoretician. He'd say, "Let me analyze the problem and let Winston solve it."

I sensed that my time at the company would eventually see its end. Once certain that I'd work for G.E. for many years, I began to think in terms of a career independent from G.E. But as the sole provider for what would become a family of five, I knew I had to proceed cautiously, so I continued working there for many years.

Oh, here's an interesting story: There was an employee strike at the plant going on one year, and I didn't want to cross the picket lines directly. It was dangerous crossing the picket lines because the Jeep was open and picketers had been known to turn vehicles over, so I thought I'd avoid doing that. So, I'd approach the plant using Buechel Bank Road and cross a wide drainage ditch with my 1946 Willys Jeep (which I still own). But on one occasion, the general manager was looking out the window and saw me. He didn't appreciate me crossing that ditch. I think he was concerned about me using an inlet to the building that wasn't normal, and they told me to stop. I honored their request.

One day, my wife Dolly shared an observation she'd made about washing machines. She said it was both a bother and very wasteful to wash small loads of delicate items inside the typical large wahing machine tub. It took a great deal of water and the large agitator would often wind delicate stockings and lingerie around the central shaft, ruining them. Dolly asked "Why isn't there a smaller basket that could hold delicate items and use less water during a shorter wash?" A great idea was born—the G.E. "Mini-basket." I refined the idea until it was just what Dolly had envisioned, a small wash basket that simply dropped down over the agitator post and

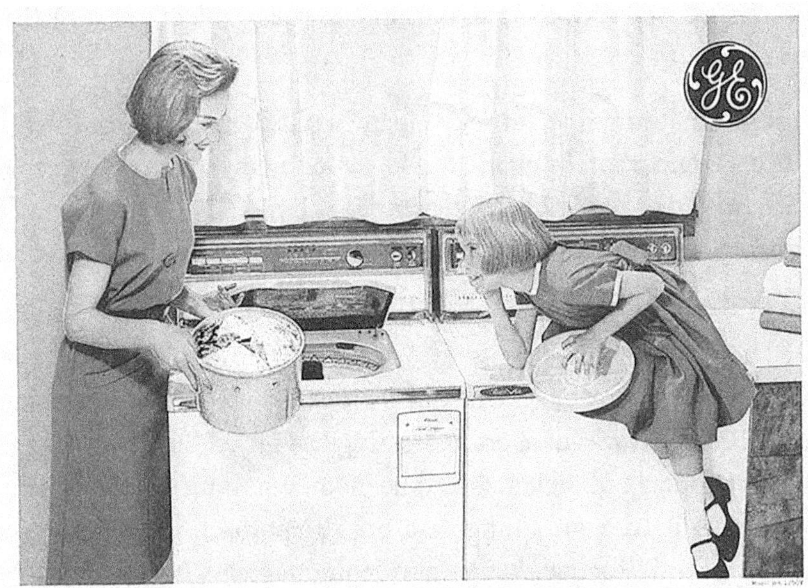

This General Electric 12-lb. washer has Mini-Basket for things you now wash by hand.

Winston made Dolly's suggestion come to life when he invented the G.E. "Mini-Basket" - "it worked like a charm!"

it worked like a charm. It could handle small two-pound loads and used one-third of the water a normal wash load required. Shelton family ingenuity moved G.E. forward again!

While still working at Appliance Park, I helped Naaman Jr., get a job in its model shop. He was so talented in that role, and I was very proud of his work. My old boss, Harold "Socks" Stocking even said to me once, "Winston, do you remember that aptitude test you took when you hired on at G.E.? Your brother made a higher grade than you. A much higher grade!" When it came to the ability to solve problems practically, "Socks" said my brother was better at it than I was. And in so far as solving mechanical problems, I can confirm he was. Eventually, Naaman Jr., was running the model shop in Building 3.

If you don't know what a model shop is, allow me to explain: It's that part of a factory devoted to building the engineering samples of a product prior to having it made for production. An engineer would take a drawing to the model shop, where they'd make a machine for us to test. Naaman, Jr., was simply outstanding in the model shop.

Winston's brother Naaman, Jr., and his wife Virginia.

I'd shared with Naaman, Jr., my frustrations with the company and confided to him that I'd like to go out on my own. We formed a plan and, a couple of years before I left G.E., we started our own company, Engineering Prototype Services, in Jeffersontown, Ky., then a Louisville suburb. Our initial aim was to develop a zero-turn radius mower, but we needed income to pursue that idea.

He had an idea: At G.E., he was forever replacing work orders for parts that were received by the thousands and needing small adjustments, things like having hole sizes increased. If G.E. had received 10,000 parts which couldn't be used without adjusting a hole size, it would send them out to a local vendor to be reworked. That's what we started doing after work hours, and we became so busy with that work, we were having trouble getting out of that business and doing what we'd intended because there was such a large need.

In the meantime, I was getting up every morning at 4 a.m. to work until "work time" on the mower. I rendered the layout and drawings that represented my design, but even as parts were being cast for the machine, we met Joe Ransdell, who was seeking engineering help on a pressure fryer he had in mind for the Kentucky Fried Chicken franchise system. He hired us to make temperature measurements on chicken then being fried in small, four-quart home pressure cookers.

Carl Mies inherited Ransdell's work, and asked our small company in 1967 to develop a pressure fryer of his description—the "Mies Fryer", which is still in production today—to allow larger batches of chicken to be fried quickly. Soon, KFC founder Colonel Sanders was on the scene, looking into what we were doing. That further took our focus off the mower and shifted me fully onto working on a pressure fryer built to the Colonel's satisfaction.

Eventually, the demands of EPS made it time for me to quit G.E. We'd become so busy that we employed five people in addition to Naaman, Jr., and me. I gave my two-week notice, though my supervisor knew a couple of years before that I'd eventually quit. (They knew about us running Engineering Prototype Services, and when they sent personnel to investigate what we were doing, we told them what we were doing.)

On my last day, it was almost as if they were happy about me leaving, though it was a cordial departure for me. They threw me a nice going away party.

After working for G.E. for 20 years, I'd begun as a level 7 engineer and become a level 13 project engineer. I was proud of what I'd done there, but I was terribly encouraged about what was happening at our company, EPS.

A Hand-built Home

For the past 62 years, Winston Shelton has lived at 5600 Chenoweth Run Road, a location once considered semi-remote until the beginning of Louisville's urban sprawl. He and wife Dolly Shelton purchased the site in 1953 for $5,000 borrowed from Dolly's father, Sylvan Stearn "Pop" Crider. Largely wooded, it was in every sense of the phrase, a country property: rustic to a degree that amused some friends and appalled others.

On the land was a tiny two-room house that had electrical power, but no running water or toilet. Initially, Winston pumped water to the two-room house from a small creek that ran alongside the property. The larger, nearby Chenoweth Creek was unfit for that purpose because it contained discharge from an upstream sewage treatment plant.

Passage from Chenoweth Run Road to the house, which was set atop a small hill, required driving the family's Willy's Jeep across Chenoweth Run, a typically tranquil stream which, from time to time was rendered impassible by steady rains or storms.

The first method Winston used to get the family across the creek to their home was named the "O S & B" (*Other Side and Back*). It was a cable stretched across the creek between two stout trees, with pulleys attached to a suspended platform hanging on the cable. The platform had a seat big enough for just one person. Using the pulleys would move the O S & B from one side of the creek to the other.

The next way Winston designed to cross the creek was what West Virginians called a "submarine": a series of 55-gallon metal drums placed on their sides, tack-welded together and overlaid with wood tracks and covered with concrete. When the design proved no match for the occasionally high water, a higher and stronger wooden bridge, spanning 25 feet and mounted to stone abutments on each bank, was built.

It, too, fell victim to high water, leading to a third and permanent single-lane bridge, designed by Winston, but this time built by a contractor, in the 1990s.

Winston and Dolly planned to build a large home in stages as the couple's brood eventually grew to three. With the help of his father and Naaman, Jr., Winston set to work on his permanent residence. The men felled timber, sawed it into boards, dug the home's foundation by hand, harvested huge stones from nearby creeks for its basement walls, and constructed a post-and-beam structure above ground.

Today, the expanses of grass and trees surrounding the home are manicured regularly by crews. Until age 93, Winston mowed the property himself, a six-hour effort he calls "pretty quick work on a zero-turn mower with a 60-inch deck." About 30 yards from the home's west-facing sun porch is a 3-acre fishing lake with grassy,

Winston and Dolly's hand-built home, circa 1962. A snowy winter scene, helping show how the house was built in the midst of their wooded Kentucky acreage.

trimmed banks. Twenty-two feet deep at one end, the lake is home to stripers, large-mouth bass and bluegill, fish caught and eaten by the Shelton family.

"When Dolly and I bought this place, we bought it for $5,000. So, we now have 40 acres of woodlands, and that's how we built this house. See those beams overhead? Dad brought his sawmill, and I got a tractor, and together, with Naaman, Jr., we cut the timber, skidded it to the mill, sawed it and built the house. We dug the stone for the foundation out of the creek.

To get the stone out of the creek … that was work! It's layered, of course, lamina on top of lamina, and you wedge between the lamina with a bar and pick it up. Sometimes when the stone was too big, you hit it with a hammer to break it to make it manageable.

I had a hydraulic platform on the back of the tractor to move the stone up the hill. Once, I put too heavy a load on back of the lift.

So, as I drove it up the hill, the front wheels of the tractor lifted up. And with those wheels in the air, I couldn't steer the tractor! Naturally, the rear differential took over. The thing began turning to the right and heading back down toward the creek—but without me! That tractor could have overturned on me, so I jumped off. I had to chase it to catch it.

The first section of our house is what has become the back section. We built it to live in. In the beginning, it wasn't much to brag about, I can tell you that. Later we extended the living room 12 feet and put in a fireplace. The stone it's made from came from the creek nearby. We extended it again to put two more bedrooms in, extended it again for the kitchen, and then, the fourth or fifth time, I don't recall, we extended it to make this room where we're sitting. … I think we're through extending! But I believe it mostly came out to reflect the original design I'd sketched. There are a few things left unfinished. I do want a cover for the patio out there. We do our entertaining there, and we like to cook out there also.

So, to go back to when we were still building … I'd go to work and share with my friends about our level of accomplishment over a particular weekend, and some said they wanted to come out to see it. Some of their wives were eager to get out into the country and see it, too. But then some of them would take a look around and soon be anxious to get away! (He laughs.) Some were truly astonished by the depravity of how we lived, but we didn't mind being laughed at. Others appreciated it, but none were as proud as we were.

Dolly was proud of what we'd done and what we were doing. That we built it ourselves was a prideful matter. It wasn't all that much fun, but I was proud to create and to use my labor.

Winston hand-built a home for his family. Here, their children Valerie, David and Laura enjoy some of the continual menagerie of pets on the stone patio, circa 1963.

How did I know how to build a house? As you can imagine, there was some study involved. Some place I learned the term "post and beam construction," and as I looked into it, I compared the work involved in sawing lumber for the home, and I quickly became more interested in making beams! It's a simpler construction than using joists for support. Beams are placed 4 feet apart rather than joists placed 16 inches apart, so in the end there's far less material and effort.

The walls are tongue-and-groove pine, and the ceilings are cork. Before we had carpet, the floors were splatter-painted concrete. The roof is all oak—really hard oak. So hard that we had to drill holes into it and screw it down instead of using nails. You couldn't drive a nail into that hard oak, so we took the easy way out.

Sometimes progress happened very slowly. That stone patio where you entered this room, Dolly said, "We have to have a better place for the kids to play." She wanted a patio. Well, getting the stone there was no problem, but filling the space between the rocks with mortar was laborious! It wasn't solid for some time, so after she'd seen too many skinned ankles on the kids, she shamed me into finishing it. That's kind of the way things progressed: I'd get the house at a level of construction that was sufficient for that point, move to something else that needed doing, and then circle back and finish the other later.

That method also didn't work out another time, when we didn't immediately put chinking and concrete between the split-pine poles on the outside walls of the house. As the winter came in, it didn't take long before we were overrun with mice! We took care to finish that project quickly!

There wasn't a lot of rest in those days. Between work and what we were doing here, I never really had a day off. I was always building something, maintaining something, always active. Like our barn out there, which is used for storage of tools and other things. When the Call-A-Mart business went broke, we bought from them the office and factory building now occupied by Winston Industries. Thirty-thousand square-feet of that building was refrigeration for groceries, and so we disassembled those refrigeration panels to make the barn. I built the grandest barn you've ever seen!

Our lake was dug in '54. I knew a man who didn't have any work for his tractor, and he dug it for me. The lake is 22 feet deep, so the dam is about 4 feet higher than that. Fishing was always a steal for me. "A steal" is what I call a lot of time away from constructive work around the property. I've enjoyed that lake immensely over the years.

The practical purpose of the lake for us was as a water source. We brought water from the lake directly to the house for bathing and washing clothes.

In the spring and the fall, the lake would "turn over," turning the water brown and murky. The water was still suitable for bathing kids but Dolly deemed it not acceptable for washing light-colored clothes. At these times of the year, Dolly would do the laundry at the laundromat.

In the summer, the lake was our favorite place to bathe. We always used Ivory soap because it floated and the girls would lather their hair with shampoo and dive from the dock, swimming underwater to rinse. Drinking water was carried from town in a 5-gallon container which we placed on a Mary Hadley pottery water dispenser that resided by the kitchen sink.

Many years later we installed a reverse osmosis filtration system. But the system was difficult to maintain. Every week I had to maintain that (filtration) membrane, washing off everything that was stuck to the back side of it ... there was so much labor involved. The filtration system fed a 500-gallon storage supply to our house and Mother and Dad's house. The water was so clean that when your car dried after washing it, there was nothing that produced graying or streaking. You didn't have to wipe it clean. When we got on city water, oh, that was a delight. But that water was never as good as the water we had before.

Was there ever a point when we just said, "It's done?" (A prolonged laugh follows.) "Not really, as we always found something else to do, something to add to our adventure.

Along the way there had been five floor plans, and with each plan came a building program and a finishing program. And it always seemed that while we were doing one, we were planning the next.

We had a lot of fun out there, and we entertained often. For a time, Dolly worked for Reynolds Aluminum, in their art department, and she had some really great friends there. So, we were constantly entertaining our G.E. and our Reynolds friends. We even had friends who wanted to get married here, so we allowed that and found ourselves with a summer and fall of entertaining those people's friends. For a while the place felt like a marriage chapel.

People loved to bring their kids over, too, and the kids would just disappear. We had three ponies that were very popular with the visiting children."

Winston now lives alone in the large home with the assistance of two women he calls his "housemothers"; one stays during the week, the other on weekends. His two dogs, Tamo and Charlie, are constant companions and ever ready to have their heads and bellies scratched. Smitten with his canine companions, he writes poems about them and posts them on a stone fireplace in his bedroom.

Next to the fireplace are a computer, two large monitors and an office chair. Networked to mirror work completed on his computer at his factory, Winston says, "Many nights I think about what I did that day, and then I consider making changes. That's why I have this set up here."

On this morning, the largest of the screens displays some recollections used in this book: time spent with his father, years served in the U.S. Army, Col. Sanders and his innovations.

From Clothes Dryers to Pressure Fryers

In 1967, Winston Shelton was a little-known engineer in a start-up company created by him and brother Naaman Shelton, Jr., to develop a zero-turn radius mower. The previous two decades of his life were spent working for G.E. making better clothes washers and dryers. Yet that same year, he was recruited to re-engineer a better pressure fryer for what would soon become the world's largest fried chicken chain.

"No, I can't say I was experienced in the area of foodservice," Winston recalls, smiling. "But boy, it was easy to see the problems with what they were doing."

"They" was Kentucky Fried Chicken, and the company's problems were multifaceted. To begin with, its chicken stores (which were then just carry-out stores, not dine-in restaurants) were challenging operations. Commonly staffed by employees 18 to 20 years old, cooks carried small, home-quality pressure cookers designed for canning from the stove to a dumping station. There, they quickly opened the pressure cooker and dumped out the pressure fried chicken and hot shortening. The blistering hot food and oil poured out onto a screen that caught the chicken and allowed the molten shortening to drip through for reuse. The constant back-and-forth carriage of hot high-pressure pots across the kitchen was no small safety concern.

The cooking process also was rudimentary. To time the heating cycle of each batch,

The official 4-quart Kentucky Fried Chicken pressure cooker pots Colonel Sanders used to cook his secret recipe chicken before the Collectramatic®.

cooks would check a wall clock and then write the start time of a batch with their fingers in the greasy film that had accumulated on the stainless-steel splash-guard behind the stoves. In busy periods, as many as 16 pots could be in use.

"Oh, those old pots—we knew there had to be a better way to cook the chicken," says Winston, who, at the time, had been hired to just evaluate a cooking timer for the pots. Producing small batches in pots, he added, rarely met demand. "The stores were always busy, so it was difficult to keep up with the number of customers that were ordering."

Around 1967, inventor Carl Mies, owner of Mies Products, had created a pressure fryer that addressed the need to cook greater volumes of chicken faster. But the fryer lacked a simple solution for filtering the bits of breading that fell off the chicken during cooking. Left in the hot shortening for extended periods, the small pieces of breading burned, sticking to the fryer's heating elements and reducing the life of the shortening. The starchy coating kept the heating element from evenly heating the oil to cook the food. It was a real mess for cooks to clean.

Winston saw an opportunity to invent an automatic filtering system attached to the bottom of the Mies design. Combining the forces of gravity and convective circulation, he knew the bits of breading would fall and collect at the bottom without clinging to the fryer's heating elements. The breading that fell off would no longer remain suspended and thus wouldn't burn in the heated shortening.

"Convection naturally occurs in the cooker as a result of the shortening being heated. When it gets hot, the shortening expands," Winston says. "As it's heated, it becomes lighter per unit area and floats upward. As it moves to the top and center of the cooker, which is further away from the heating elements mounted at the sides of the cooker, it cools, gets heavier and flows downward and outward where it's reengaged by the heaters."

Since the Mies design did not filter automatically, cooks had to shut it off and drain the shortening and filter it manually. By contrast, Winston's collector allowed for continuous, automatic filtration and long, uninterrupted periods of operation.

"I said to myself, 'If it's going to flow to the bottom already, let's give it a chance to go to the bottom of the collector instead of just the bottom of the fryer," Winston says.

The device worked so well that KFC store operators initially didn't believe it succeeded so simply, so they put it to the test—by cooking 20 batches of chicken without stopping.

Winston and the Colonel in front of a US map showing the cities where the early Collectramatic fryers were being used in KFC stores.

"Then, when they took off that collector, they'd find it packed with all that fall-off," he says.

No one was more pleased with the invention than KFC founder, Col. Harland Sanders. For him, Winston's collector achieved the goal of filtering the hot shortening while cooking, and providing the prized "cracklins" he insisted be used to make chicken gravy according to his notoriously high standards.

"When he saw it, he said, 'My God, Lynn (he was so excited, the Colonel called Winston by the wrong name), you've really got something there!'" Winston recalls. "Then, he said, 'My goodness, look what I have to make my gravy from!'"

Believing a sales bonanza would follow the Colonel's endorsement, Winston was faced with having to move quickly to construct a manufacturing team and assembly system. He hired two dozen people, many of whom had worked in the G.E. model shop, including Lew Newman.

"He became a plant manager over here and started hiring additional people at G.E. to work here," Winston recalls. "We used people to improve upon people and hired skilled professionals. That led us to demand a little more of ourselves and thereby demand a little bit more of the other person. We built a really good team pretty quickly."

With the first 16 Collectramatics made, Winston put them to the test, watching the fryers cycle on and off for a week to prove they worked.

Winston's Collectramatic fryer. The round cylinder at the bottom of the unit is the collector.

"Then we quickly shipped them out to earn some income from them!" he says, grinning. "Ours was a start-up. We really needed the money!"

As word of the self-filtering pressure cooker (eventually named the Collectramatic®) raced through the KFC franchise system, orders flowed back to Louisville with alacrity. When a new store using Collectramatics opened, KFC franchisees from nearby towns came to see them in action.

"Pete Harmon, the Colonel's first franchisee, would open a store in Utah, and three to four franchisees would show up to watch," he says. "They'd see how well it worked, and I'd go back home and receive orders from them."

A 2012 *Louisville* magazine article quoted former KFC purchasing vice president and franchisee, Fred Jeffries, crediting the Collectramatic for boosting per-store sales more than four-fold.

"'Stores were doing about $200,000 a year in sales on average with the pots . . . but they could never have done the $900,000 a year it became without Win's fryer,'" Jefferies told the magazine. "He helped set the stage for that with true engineering thinking."

Word of mouth among KFC franchisees sold the Collectramatic without any advertising. According to Winston, they were a close fraternity of operators who trusted each other.

"Those franchisees stuck together and told each other of their successes, of what they were doing and what worked," he says. "That sold the Collectramatic within that chain."

But not within the corporation itself. John Y. Brown, Jr., one of two men who bought Kentucky Fried Chicken from Sanders in 1964, had made an exclusive arrangement with franchisee L.S. Hartzog to supply an automatic chicken fryer of his creation for KFC corporate-owned stores. Winston learned of the arrangement at a

KFC franchisee convention in the early 1970s.

"L.S. walked over and asked if I thought KFC would approve my cooker," he begins. (To ensure consistency of product throughout a system, franchise companies commonly approve a limited range of equipment for use in their stores.) "I told him I believed they would, yet he told me was certain they wouldn't because they had a contract with him."

Hartzog said the contract bound KFC to pay him $300 for any non-Hartzog cooker brought into the KFC system. Surprised by the arrangement, Winston summoned the Colonel, who was nearby, and had Hartzog explain the deal to him.

"Even the Colonel said it was the first time he'd heard about it," Winston says.

Equally surprising to Winston was the cost of a Hartzog fryer: $16,000 for a machine that could cook "20 heads at a time," meaning 180 pieces of chicken cut to the Colonel's unique nine-piece standard. By comparison, a Collectramatic cost about $1,500, and fried six heads (54 pieces) at a time.

"An operator could buy four Collectramatics for $6,000 and outdo the 20-head cooker that cost $16,000. The 20-head Hartzog cooker still needed to be backed up by one or two other smaller fryers," Winston begins. "On slower days, you could run just one or two Collectramatics as needed. My design was much more effective and efficient than the Hartzog design." Given volume discounts for Collectramatic purchases, multistore KFC operators often bought more than they needed to get the lowest price, and then resold their extra cookers to smaller franchisees.

"We were selling them like crazy, just smoking them!" Winston recalls. When working at capacity, Collectramatics could be ordered, manufactured and shipped to a domestic KFC operator in as quickly as 10 days. "And KFC owed Hartzog $300 more every time we sold one into the system. It was bloody, man!"

Aware it was in a costly contractual fix, KFC sought to stanch that bleeding. KFC senior vice president, Norm Haberman, reached out to Winston to discuss how to resolve the problem. With a corporate attorney beside him, Haberman gauged Winston's willingness to sell his company to KFC. If owned by the chicken chain and made part of "the system," the payouts to Hartzog would end. Sensing an advantage, yet ultimately desiring to keep his business, Winston told Haberman that he'd sell for $20 million, an astounding sum for a small firm in 1971.

"I knew our company was worth maybe $1 million at the time, but I wasn't just going to hand it over to them," he recalls. "That they wanted to buy Collectramatic at all proved its value as a cooker, but also proved their disdain for me at KFC. They wanted to solve 'their Winston problem' by buying me out. But that didn't happen."

Without a deal, the cycle of Collectramatic sales and Hartzog payouts continued until food and beverage giant Heublein bought KFC off the public market and placed it under private ownership. With Brown now out as KFC's president, Barry Rowles, his replacement under Heublein, visited Winston to discuss how to end the matter.

"By that point, we'd sold thousands of Collectramatics into the system, and they'd paid L.S. $300 for every one of them," Winston recalls. "Eventually Rowles knew he had to satisfy L.S. somehow to end the arrangement, which is what happened."

Instead of buying Collectramatic from Winston, Heublein bought Hart Biscuit Co. from L.S. Hartzog, and the 20-head cooker along with it. "That settled the matter, though I was never privy to the terms of that deal," Winston says. To Rowles' credit and to Winston's advantage, however, the Collectramatic was now approved for the KFC system.

Unfortunately, that wasn't the only battle faced by Winston's fledgling Collectramatic company during its early years. A banker with whom Winston did business was found not only misappropriating Collectramatic's funds, he had also convinced Winston to sign for a $50,000 business loan *and* buy a $38,000 aircraft.

"Our company was quite young, so to get a loan of that size with so little cash inflow revealed a problem," Winston recalls.

Arthur Brown, a retired executive of the bank was asked to investigate the issue, and he started with Winston. Realizing that the engineer wasn't aware the funds weren't properly accounted for, or knowledgeable about the peculiarities of the loan and the aircraft purchase, he believed Winston wasn't at fault.

"He concluded I wasn't involved in a conspiracy, but that I was indeed a little naïve," Winston says. "The (fraudulent) banker was later indicted, but the day he was to appear in court on charges, he was found dead in his shower."

While his bank viewed Winston's naïveté as honest and understandable, it still wanted its money. After reselling the aircraft, it pressed Winston on how he'd repay the $50,000 loan. Short on cash, he turned to his old friend, Colonel Sanders for help. When

Arthur Brown and Winston met with the founder of Kentucky Fried Chicken, the Colonel agreed to cosign on Winston's note for the debt—under one condition:

"That I'd sell him the rights to sell my Collectramatic cooker into the KFC system in Canada for $50,000," Winston says.

Winston and Colonel Sanders.

The shrewdness of Sander's maneuver wasn't lost on Winston, who knew that Sanders had not sold the Kentucky Fried Chicken franchise rights for Canada to John Y. Brown, Jr., and Jack Massey, when they bought his company a decade before.

"That he stood in for me and showed his confidence in me, that was the most important thing," Winston says. "The Colonel's reputation for being cantankerous was appropriately deserved. But he also could be inexplicably generous."

Sanders stood in for Winston and the Collectramatic on other occasions when money got tight, making appearances before key suppliers to give his equipment a tacit endorsement of quality and potential. John Demy, owner of Louisville Machinery, and one of Winston's largest suppliers, got tense when Winston's payments for tools and manufacturing supplies slowed down. Leaning on the

Colonel's cachet and a few well-placed friends at G.E., Winston convinced Demy to continue to both supply the company and offer him credit when necessary.

Starting a small business with large capital requirements was difficult, Winston recalls, and his solution to keeping suppliers happy was to visit them personally and convince them all would work out.

"The Colonel was such a tremendous help to me. He used to stop in and ask, 'Winston, are you having any trouble at any place?'" Winston says. "And sometimes I'd say, 'Yes, I am. Could you take a trip with me?' And the Colonel would say to a supplier, 'Winston is helping me,' which implied they should help me.

"We personalized it, which you have to do when you're the new kid on the block with a company named Collectramatic, and nobody knows what that is. You always need help."

Sanders' own expectations that the Collectramatic would sell well came true. Sales of the fryer made an eleven-fold leap from a meager $74,211 in 1970 to $852,233 in 1971. Revenue tripled the next year to almost $2.5 million, before jumping again to more than $3.6 million in 1973. It took the OPEC-initiated oil crisis of 1974 to cool sales to $2.5 million, though the company remained profitable.

"You'd get on a turnpike and see nobody traveling," Winston says, recalling that year when the U.S. government printed gasoline ration stamps, but never issued them. "We made machines, a lot of them, but nobody was buying them as much."

An engineer to the core, Winston relied on his former G.E. engineering peers to help him test and improve the Collectramatic's design and performance. One of them was Gene Pottinger, who assisted in design modifications and shared patents for the machine with Winston. The two men later founded a spice and blending and breading company named Blendex, which Pottinger eventually took over.

Another G.E. alum was Leo Loeb, an engineer Winston relied on to test the Collectramatic's performance, as well as future equipment invented by Winston Industries.

"Now, let me tell you, Leo Loeb was the finest scientist I've ever known," Winston says. "I wanted to hire him over here ... because we'd worked so well together in the past. He was all business, a smart man who was serious about his work. And he was very helpful in both the development of Collectramatic and, later, the CVap."

Since the Collectramatic's creation more than four decades ago, Winston estimates sales of the revolutionary pressure fryer add up to around $150 million—a more-than-tidy sum for a man who left G.E. to prototype an advanced lawnmower that never got built. Since then, nearly 64,000 Collectramatics have been sold to food-service operations in 130 countries. On trips to some of those destinations, Winston has found some of the earliest releases of the fryer still in action.

"In 2011, I was in Kuala Lumpur at a store where they had some of the first fryers I'd sold internationally in the '70s, and they were still in use!" he says.

That they're still in use isn't surprising he says, since durability was essential to his initial design. When creating them, he insisted on fabricating all its parts from high-quality metals instead of sourcing lower-grade market-ready pieces. "They were still cooking with them every day, but, my goodness, they had kept them in such nice shape! ... To see that, well, it made me just so damn proud of what we'd done."

Perhaps not surprisingly, he regards the Collectramatic as his favorite invention "because of the engineering required for the structure to endure the pressure." Adding with a broad grin, he says, "I do rather like it."

Barry Yates, global accounts manager at Winston Industries, has worked with and traveled extensively with Winston, and tells stories of countless impromptu stops to see restaurants that caught the pair's fancy. The thrill of finding a piece of Winston Industries equipment in those kitchens has yet to get old, he says.

"Once, on a road trip through Indiana, we both saw a road sign for skillet-fried chicken, and without saying much of anything, we knew we were going to pull over and see if it really was skillet-fried chicken," Barry says. "Of course, we figured out that it wasn't, but it was really good chicken, so we had a hunch it was ours. Turns out, yes, they were using a Collectramatic."

A Paint and Canvas Homage to Colonel Sanders

Winston Shelton wasn't the only person to idolize Colonel Harland Sanders. Winston's wife, Dolly, had a keen understanding of how profoundly KFC's founder had helped her husband's fledgling business and, ultimately, her family. What surprised Winston was what Dolly was prepared to do to demonstrate that gratitude.

One morning in 1973, she startled Winston by suggesting they honor Sanders with a portrait painted by Norman Rockwell, the famed artist who'd painted countless covers for the "Saturday Evening Post," then just a magazine. It was a serious and significant request, as Rockwell's portraits included legendary faces such as actors Spencer Tracy and Bob Hope, and U.S. Presidents Eisenhower, Kennedy, Johnson and Nixon. Dolly believed wholeheartedly that Sanders' visage deserved equal treatment to theirs.

"When she told me she wanted Rockwell to do it, I told her, 'I thought he was dead,'" Winston recalls with a laugh. "She said, 'No, I just saw him riding a bike on television,' so I knew then I'd better get to work reaching out to him."

Winston asked then marketing manager George Bemis to write Rockwell and ask him to accept the commission to paint Colonel Sanders. The artist declined due to work he was busy completing for the nation's bicentennial then a year or so away. Undeterred, Winston sent Rockwell a check, but found it returned promptly with a note saying he did not take fees in advance. Winston continued the correspondence until Rockwell relented and invited him, Dolly, Sanders and his wife, Claudia, to his Stockbridge, Massachusetts studio, where a photographer would take reference shots.

Rockwell's modest studio was housed in a barn once owned by the U.S.'s most infamous traitor, Benedict Arnold. Painted deep red, Winston recalls the frame building as home to countless finished and unfinished art works, a potbellied stove and the many tools of Rockwell's trade.

He recalls Rockwell as kind and polite, and says he consulted him and Dolly on how they wanted Sanders' image painted. Their muse included children in the image, but Rockwell disagreed, saying the portrait needed to focus on the main subject.

"I don't recall exactly whether he called me persistent or insistent, but he wasn't being critical," Winston recalls. "It was as if to say, 'You wouldn't be here unless you had stuck with it like you did.'"

Winston recalls Rockwell—then 80 years old—as a man of modest frame and sloping shoulders, "and I noticed one of his feet was somewhat turned in. It caused him to walk with a noticeable limp." (In a 1980 *Christian Science Monitor* article titled, "Norman Rockwell collection; He painted us all," David Wood, a friend of Rockwell's, said the artist was humorously self-effacing about being pigeon-toed and knock-kneed, claiming, "My brother was the athlete. I was a real klutz.")

When Sanders was seated to pose for the photographer, Rockwell said to the shooter, "Look at him, isn't he beautiful!" Winston says he understood Rockwell's appreciation of Sander's extraordinary looks.

Norman Rockwell's 1973 portrait of Colonel Sanders.

"The Colonel had a pink, robust face, especially for someone his age," Winston begins. "That pinkness did not symbolize weakness, it was a strong face, not to mention the fact that he had beautiful silver hair. And when the Colonel heard what Rockwell said, he was kind of proud and puffed up. They related well to each other that afternoon and had a friendly chat."

By 1975, the portrait was finished and was to be sent to the KFC National Franchisee Convention in Las Vegas, Nevada. But when the portrait arrived, their eyes were riveted to a most noticeable flaw: Rockwell had painted Sanders wearing only the bow portion of Sander's trademark Kentucky Colonel string bowtie. To any fan of the Colonel, the mistake was akin to painting a pope wearing a

Colonel Sanders, his wife Claudia, Winston and Dolly Shelton, Norman Rockwell, daughter Laura Shelton, Dick Miller (Colonel Sanders' driver) and son David Shelton at Rockwell's studio in Stockbridge, Massachussetts.

baseball cap.

We told Rockwell it wouldn't do, that it had to be fixed," Winston says, "We paid $8,000 for it so we wanted it fixed."

With the KFC convention only days away, the decision was made to have daughter Valerie fly the painting back to Stockbridge to have Rockwell finish the painting. Two airline seats were purchased: one for Valerie and one for the portrait. Upon arrival at the Rockwell studio, Rockwell seemed to have forgotten the appointment but with a nudge from his assistant, Rockwell allowed Valerie and the painting in. Valerie, armed with a photo of the Colonel, pointed out the oversight with the painting. Rockwell announced that he could not paint in the strings because the oil paint would not dry for 3 days. He finally took a pencil, sketched in the string portions of the tie and dismissed Valerie with instructions to have a local artist paint them in.

Winston's wife Dolly called on Warren "Bud" Dillen, a friend who was an artist at Reynolds Aluminum, where she worked. Dillen said he'd be honored to fix it, and called Rockwell to discuss masking the miscue.

"Later, when it was finished, I talked to Bud about how he did it, and he said he studied some of Rockwell's work so he could try and duplicate his strokes," Winston says. "When I looked at it, I couldn't tell that it had been changed. He did a remarkable job."

Corrected satisfactorily, the painting was taken to the convention and displayed. Upon seeing the portrait, the Colonel deemed it beautiful and dubbed Rockwell "a genius."

For some time, the portrait hung in Winston's office and his home. In the summer of 2006, Winston gave the portrait to daughter Valerie, who then placed it on loan to KFC from the Shelton Family. The portrait currently hangs in a Sanders' tribute room at the KFC headquarters in Louisville, Kentucky.

In total, 5,000 prints were made of the original painting and most were given to KFC franchisees. According to Winston, Sanders personalized one for him that reads, "'To my dear friend.' It looks down on me at my desk, reminding me of his friendship and reminding me of my commitment to his idea."

From an Ideal Holding Cabinet to Revolutionary Ovening

CONTROLLED VAPOR TECHNOLOGY®

For decades, restaurant operators and equipment manufacturers tried in vain to hold fried chicken in an optimal serving condition after cooking. Holding it in a heated cabinet did preserve the crust texture, but it eventually dried out the meat. Using moist heat threatened the opposite outcome of a soggy exterior.

In the late 1970s, Winston Shelton discovered the solution: Holding fried chicken perfectly cooked for extended periods could not be done using one type of heat. Instead, it took a careful combination of moist and dry heat sources. This breakthrough centered on the understanding that since all food is mostly water, using water vapor as a heat transfer agent could keep it hot without drying it out. Drying and texturing exterior food surfaces (such as that on fried chicken) could be done with a dry heat source. That breakthrough led to the creation of what Winston later named Controlled Vapor Technology, and was manifested in his CVap® ovening device.

Harland Sanders and Winston Shelton were an ideal match as business associates. One was obsessed with the quality of his fried chicken, the other with making machines that helped the other realize that goal. Yet despite the great advances in cooking Kentucky Fried Chicken made by Winston's Collectramatic Pressure Fryer, "holding" that perfectly fried chicken in a just-cooked, ready-to-eat state was a stiff challenge.

In restaurant argot, "holding" is when a kitchen staff cooks about 10 percent to 20 percent more food than needed at a given time. Having food ready and "holding" it allows the kitchen to stay a step ahead of customers wanting food quickly when they arrive.

In the 1970s, food cooked in advance was held in heated metal cabinets, and operators struggled to maintain the ideal moist and hot qualities of perfectly cooked food. This was especially true for the Colonel's pressure fried chicken, which when held, could dry out to the point it couldn't be served after about 20 minutes.

The fact the Colonel wanted to hold fried chicken made matters doubly difficult because of that dish's long cook time. Even cooked under pressure, a batch of fried chicken requires 15 to 25 minutes to finish. And as fast-food soared in popularity in the 1970s, few customers would wait that long at a carryout window.

The problem preoccupied Colonel Sanders' mind often, and on a trip to Cincinnati, Winston recalls him thinking aloud about it.

"I heard him say, almost absentmindedly, 'I wish my chicken could be held a little closer to New Orleans than Denver,'" Winston recalls. "I think he was thinking something out loud and not really speaking to me. But it was clear he was saying he wanted a different climate in which to hold his cooked chicken."

"Climate," in this case, is an especially significant term. Like Sanders, Winston understood that the humid air surrounding New Orleans would make an ideal microclimate inside a holding cabinet—the very spot where his food quickly became "Denver dry."

"It wasn't immediately apparent how to fix the problem, but what was clear to me was the standard holding cabinets the industry used were problematic from the start," Winston says. "They were poorly suited for what the Colonel felt he *needed*. He really cared that his food be perfect."

Eager to help his friend, Winston set out to understand the shortcomings inherent in cooked food holding cabinets of that era, most of which used electric heating elements that created dry heat. Worse, if not correctly vented, moisture evaporated out of the food would turn the food within the cabinet soggy.

Further tests revealed a valuable insight: Though the air temperature inside the cabinet held steady at 180° F, the food's temperature never reached the temperature at which the cabinet was set. While air temperature in the cabinet was well controlled, food temperature wasn't. And as the food within evaporated its internal moisture, it cooled itself off instead of heating up.

Studying the matter further, he acknowledged that since all food is mostly water, it was, in scientific terms, a "wet body." Therefore, heating foods in a way that kept wet bodies from losing moisture had to involve water. Further study led him to understand that water heated to a vapor state had a remarkable ability to convey its heat to other bodies. Better yet, he learned that heated water was 20 times more effective at conveying heat to other bodies than heated air.

"When we heat water and its vapor pressure increases, the heated water vapor pushes out to everything else nearby with a lower vapor pressure in order to transfer its heat to it," Winston says. "This happens exactly as it does in nature."

As in New Orleans, to be exact. Located beside Lake Pontchartrain in South Louisiana, the Crescent City is notoriously humid during summer due to the environment's access to water from the lake, the Mississippi River and the Gulf of Mexico. Heated by the sun, water from those massive wet bodies vaporizes into the air, touching other wet bodies—most notably humans—making them sweaty and uncomfortable as the water vapor conveys more heat to their bodies.

By contrast, Denver, located 5,000 feet above sea level in the Rocky Mountains and far away from large bodies of water, has a dry climate. And without a boundless supply of water to vaporize into the air, an 85° F day in Denver is dryer and feels far more comfortable than an 85° F day in humid New Orleans.

Essential to all of this, Winston says, was understanding the difference between "dry bulb" and "wet bulb" temperatures: "Dry bulb" temperature is a measurement of heat content in air, and a dry bulb thermometer's bulb is bare. A wet bulb thermometer is influenced by the combination of heat in the air along with moisture vapor present in the air. To measure this combination, the bulb on a wet bulb thermometer is covered with a wet cloth.

"In terms of weather, for instance, dry bulb tells you only the temperature of the air itself," Winston says. "Wet bulb tells you the temperature relative to the amount of moisture present in the air."

Winston theorized that the temperature differential between wet bulb and dry bulb temperatures could provide the solution to the Colonel's desire to keep his chicken hot and moist on the inside and not drying out while being held for sale. He knew that controlling wet and dry bulb temperatures separately and specifically would be essential to acheiveing that aim.

Winston then created a prototype to test his theory using a standard food holding cabinet fitted with a basic evaporator made from a pan of water placed at the unit's bottom. The evaporator was also fitted with a heating element and a thermostat. He then set a wet bulb temperature target to replicate the moist, hot atmospheric conditions of New Orleans, and a dry bulb target using the cabinet's standard heating elements. He felt the latter would maintain the fresh-fried texture of the chicken's crust.

To his delight, the experiment was a success!

The food's temperature was controlled precisely by managing the water vapor temperature (wet bulb), and the texture of the chicken's exterior was controlled by the temperature differential, i.e. the difference between the air temperature (dry bulb) and the water temperature. According to Winston, the temperature differential during those chicken tests was roughly 30° F (i.e. a 150° F wet bulb setting and a 180°F dry bulb setting.) Within that temperature gap, he says, is where you can control how and when food moisture evaporates.

Winston named the new "Controlled Vapor Technology," which

later was shortened to CVap, and defined thusly: Controlled Vapor Technology is the management of one heat source to 1. control food temperature without the loss of food moisture; and 2. manage a second heat source to control food moisture without affecting food temperature.

Applied to the proper way of holding fried chicken: If a chef wants no exterior texturing of food, such as when cooking vegetables, the differential temperature will be set to 0° F. In this example, the air within the CVap will be highly moisture laden (New Orleans).

If a chef wants significant texturing, such as for baking, the differential temperature will be set to the opposite extreme in the 50° F to 100° F range (very dry, such as Denver). Texturing and/or browning (known in culinary circles as the Maillard effect) begins when food temperatures reach the temperature of the evaporator.

With the help of research scientist Leo Loeb, Winston tested, tweaked and improved his understanding of the prototype to view it as a low-temperature "ovening" cabinet—no longer a mere food holding cabinet. By 1977, he invited Sanders to the factory to see his finished prototype. Winston showed him the 180° F dry bulb and 150° F wet bulb settings and explained the value of the temperature differential. Then he let the Colonel sample fried chicken he'd held perfectly for more than two hours.

"He was amazed by it!" Winston recalls. "Sadly, though, he passed away (in 1980) before he could see the final product at work. Still, I'm quite satisfied we achieved what he had desired for so long."

But as Winston took the product to potential fast-food chain customers, not everyone was as thrilled. They didn't understand the

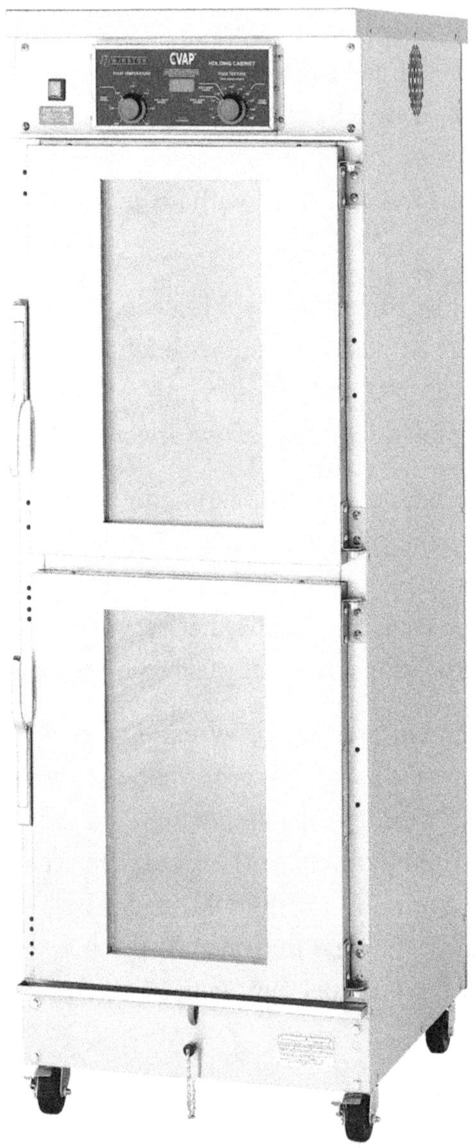

The oven that started a revolution in the foodservice industry around the world - Winston Shelton's "Controlled Vapor Oven®" - the CVap®.

new process. KFC's then head of research and development, Dr. G.V. Rao, was among them. According to Winston, when Rao opened the cabinet's door and saw a cloud of water vapor rush out, he simply walked away.

"He left me standing there in his laboratory without investigating it," Winston says, shrugging his shoulders. "But we did sell some CVaps to loyal KFC franchisees."

Sometime later, McDonald's reached out to Winston to order CVaps for a sausage biscuit sandwich rollout. But as he began to ship orders, he was summoned to the burger giant's headquarters near Chicago for a troubling meeting.

"The problem, as it was explained to me, was (McDonald's chairman) Ray Kroc had promised several suppliers they could have certain portions of McDonald's business, and I wasn't among them," Winston recalls. "I was told the rest of what was a large order for CVaps would be cancelled."

Wendy's Old-Fashioned Hamburgers later stepped up in a big way, buying many CVaps for use on an array of the chain's products. Later, school systems became customers.

"I was in Atlanta at a school foodservice show, and a woman walked up to me and said, 'Are you Winston? Let me tell you a story,'" Winston begins. "She said, 'Pizza is both the best day and the worst day in school foodservice, because the kids love it, but because we have always had trouble delivering it at the quality we should.'"

A CVap, she explained, solved her pizza problem immediately.

"'So, I bought one of your CVaps and tried it one day on a pizza,'" Winston recalls. "'And after a 1-hour period of holding, I couldn't believe my eyes. It was as though it was just cooked.' She then said she was buying CVaps for all her applications."

Ever-bent toward constant improvement, Winston not only continued perfecting CVap, he vigorously pursued his studies of cooking with vapor to fully understand the science behind it. While he knew the ovening device was an exceptional holding cabinet, he was getting new feedback from chefs using the device solely for cooking. Noteworthy in their remarks was the significant food yields the new controlled vapor cooking process provided, especially when compared to product losses encountered in dry-heat ovening, which drew moisture out of foods.

"As we studied the matter of yield further, our own research agreed with what culinarians were telling us," Winston begins, "and that was CVap increased yield in certain foods by as much as 40 percent! When you cook food with vapor, it cannot give up its own moisture. So, when that moisture is retained, you're keeping the natural juices in a beef roast or a turkey, as well as the moisture within vegetables. That equates to greater flavor and succulence in the food served to the customer, and vastly improved food cost for the chef."

Perhaps most surprising to Winston was the eventual praise CVap earned from some of the nation's top chefs. At an American Culinary Federation meeting in Las Vegas, a chef approached the Winston Industries booth to investigate a large, steaming beef roast on display. When the chef requested Winston cut the roast down the middle, the chef was captivated by the top-to-bottom uniformity of perfectly cooked, bright pink beef.

"Then he said, 'Now cut just the end off of it,' thinking he'd see something different, and so I cut it," Winston says. When the chef noticed that it also was uniformly bright pink, he said, "'Oh my! It's the same color on the end as in the middle!'"

Later, the chef returned with another colleague to see the beef. He said to Winston, "'Tell this chef how you did that, how you got rid of the usual dark ring of color on the outside edge of the sliced beef,'" Winston recalls. He explained to the chefs that a conventional dry-heat oven dehydrates the outer edge of the roast and discolors it. Using low-temperature water vapor to cook, however, allowed the CVap to render the roast perfectly pink from edge to edge. "They were really impressed to see that."

Winston says that by the new millennia, praise for "how grandly we held fried chicken or mashed potatoes with CVap" was being drowned out by accolades from an increasing number of headliner chefs across America.

"The things they were doing with it were beyond anything we'd ever imagined," he says. "In that respect, they were teaching me!"

Barry Yates, global accounts manager at Winston and a career chef, cited "CVap Staging" as one technique becoming widely used by restaurant chefs who own CVap Cook & Hold ovens and CVap Holding cabinets and drawers. Using CVap's low-temperature cooking abilities, they could heat proteins to a precise temperature and doneness, and then hold them fully cooked, to be "finished" to a diner's order.

"That way you add the aesthetic properties at the end, which is backward from how I was trained to cook as a chef," Yates began. In other words, a cut of beef can be CVap staged to rare or medium-rare doneness, and when ordered, charred quickly on a grill or in a pan and served uniformly pink inside to the guest. "We're teaching people now that you don't have to cook and caramelize at the same time. Even after all these years of people doing it, it's still seen by many as a radical approach to cooking."

Dean Corbett, chef-owner of Equus in Louisville, Ky., cooks lobster tails in a CVap and sees ultra-tender results.

"I cook them in lobster stock in the CVap at 95 degrees and just take it super slow," he says. "They come out so tender, it's unreal. You can't do that by steaming it or grilling it."

Kevin Nashan, chef-owner of multiple St. Louis, Mo., restaurants, including Sidney St. Café and Four Hands, agrees with Corbett, saying CVap is an extraordinary tool for cooking shellfish.

"When you cook mussels, you want the customer to experience that same bite as you get right when it opens in the pan," says Nashan, a 2017 James Beard Award winner for "Best Chef, Midwest." "But that's difficult to do when you have 30 of them on order."

"So, we heat them on the stove like you'd normally do, and as they pop open, we just put them into a CVap to hold perfectly until it's time to serve them."

Contrary to most kitchens, where chefs hold sauces heated to serving temperature in steam wells, Nashan holds them in a CVap, "because they don't reduce just sitting there, and they never form a skin on top, which is just incredible. ... We also use one of our CVaps to ferment sausages. It's an amazing tool in so many ways."

Alex Talbot, a Plumstead, Pa., chef and consultant with Ideas in Food, calls CVap revolutionary for its ability to "fine-tune" the exact outcome he wants from his food.

"We're able to cook with it and then pinpoint our observations because everything is done in slow motion," says Talbot, who has worked with CVaps for 11 years. "It allows us to look at exact temperatures and say, 'I like the result when I do this.' We use CVap a lot for its ability to do controlled cooking at low temperatures, but it also does really well for holding a burger. It can do just about whatever you want it to do when you work to understand how it cooks."

From Manufacturing to Fried Chicken Franchising

In the development of Collectramatic and CVap, Winston Shelton fried countless batches of chicken. Learning how to make and hold fried chicken correctly amounted to a level of skill he deduced was directly applicable to the marketplace as a fried chicken franchisor.

Still, Winston was no fool. Kentucky Fried Chicken, one of his key customers, dominated the restaurant industry's fast-food chicken segment sold at freestanding operations, so there was no point in going head to head. Instead, he looked for an underserved niche opportunity, settling on convenience stores, service stations and grocery delicatessens that could benefit from the top-line sales boost hot, fresh food would provide. The idea also was rooted in the Cross Roads Restaurant and Service Station owned by his parents years before.

Since such sites weren't traditional restaurants, he realized he would have to invent a pressure fryer able to function without the required and costly exhaust hoods. He'd also have to provide franchisees breading for their fried chicken, and branding materials that would make his fried chicken a readily and memorably identifiable brand.

The fryer he created was named the "Condensomat." Largely a Collectramatic, it was equipped with a unique system that condensed the shortening that had been vaporized by the intense heat of the fryer. Instead of venting the vaporized shortening into the air for release through an exhaust hood, it was exhausted into a tank through which impeller-driven water condensed the vaporized shortening.

"The Condensomat consumed the vapors that would have been exhausted normally into the room. It worked without a hood," Winston says. The breading, he added, was the creation of "a flavor expert we worked with named Jack Davis. He was an amazing talent. I think what he created was even a little bit better even than KFC."

By 1986 52 district sales representatives (DSRs) spread throughout the U.S. and Winston Industries began signing on franchisees of two food concepts. The first was *"Fancy Fried Chicken."* The second was *"Opal & Naaman Shelton's Original Crossroads Restaurant Recipe Country Fried Chicken,"* that name an homage to his parents. It didn't take long before new franchisees were ordering Condensomats and getting into the chicken business.

Fancy Fried Chicken made quick inroads into grocery and C-stores; and Opal & Naaman Shelton's Original Crossroads Restaurant Recipe Country Fried Chicken was both a stand alone restaurant concept as well as an adjunct to convenience stores. It served side items along with its chicken.

"It took off, man, and we were on to something," Winston says.

A Fancy Fried Chicken banner in a mid-west convenience store. Winston's self-serve chicken merchandiser is on the left below the banner, next to the customer.

"With all of the side items, Opal and Naaman's was more of a fast-food adjunct than Fancy Fried," Winston recalls.

In addition to selling Condensomat fryers, Winston Industries' dry-ingredient blending company, Blendex, sold packaged breading to each client.

"The breading was a good margin item for us," Winston says. "All of those things gave our salesmen new things to sell. It provided some great opportunities for them and us."

Yeager's Key Market, located in Jeffersontown, Ky., and conveniently along Winston's drive home from the factory, bought four

The Opal & Naaman Shelton's Country Fried Chicken logo featured line drawings of Winston's mother and father.

Condensomat fryers in the early 1990s. According to Jeff Stegner, who managed the broad-line grocery store back then, sales of Opal and Naaman's fried chicken were always brisk.

"We'd sell it right out of the fryer to customers because often we just couldn't keep up," Stegner says. "If we held it, it was 15 minutes at the most. I'm telling you, it was darn good chicken."

During the annual Jeffersontown Gaslight Festival in 1992—the busiest weekend of the year for Yeager's—Stegner recalls one of his four fryers quit working and left him desperate to get it fixed. Knowing the part he needed, he called Winston Industries for help. "Apparently Winston was at home cutting his grass, and somebody called him about the part we needed," Stegner says. "He went to the factory himself, got the part and brought it to us. I never forgot that. It was a class operation, and Winston had the best equipment."

David George was manager of customer service at Winston Industries during that period, and he recalls the success of the new fried chicken concepts. Winston, he says, was particularly proud of being able to name one of them after his parents.

"It meant so much to Win because he loved his family so much,"

George says. "He really wanted to do something for them and about them."

As Winston recalls, there were as many as 500 installations of his company's chicken concepts across the nation, though Barry Yates believes the number may have actually been double that. Either way, Winston's sales were on a meteoric rise.

"Those chicken sales really produced business for those service stations and small stores," Winston says. Yet despite both concepts' success, Winston began to have misgivings about his ventures into fried chicken sales.

"The project eventually proved a tough choice for me about whether I needed to be in the fried chicken business against my best customers," Winston says. "We quickly moved to discontinue our part of the chicken business because of the objections of those franchisees. They'd been good to us for a lot of years and we certainly owed them that respect."

But that wasn't the only challenge faced by the new fried chicken concepts. Blendex and Winston Industries were operating under the same roof. There was a health risk of cross-contamination of food products made within a durable goods manufacturing facility. The local health board's ruling: shut down Blendex or relocate it.

"So we sold the Blendex company to Gene Pottinger," Winston says. At that time, Pottinger owned 10 percent of Winston Industries, and the two simplified the deal with Pottinger returning his shares of the company back to Winston. (Blendex still provides ingredients to the foodservice industry and is located a short distance from Winston Industries.)

George says he was sad to see the company's chicken operations end, but not as sad as Winston.

"It broke my heart for Winston when they decided to shut it all down," says George, who serviced many Condensomats. "He had a lot of pride in them, and it was something different for him. And I can tell you, Winston's chicken really was good!"

Thinking...
Inside "The Room"

Authors' note: Throughout our many interviews with Winston, he frequently mentioned his mental exercise of "going into a room" in which he envisioned solutions to problems that were actual or anticipated. We were intrigued by the practice and believed readers also would be interested, so we asked him to explain how he "enters" his room of discovery and invention.

Winston discussed the mental process of "getting inside" machinery, where he could examine its working parts and understand on a micro-scale the causes of certain conditions or problems, their effects on the whole machine, and the potential outcomes of changing it.

While an engineer at G.E. he entered "the room" to understand why the suspension on an early model washing machine didn't effectively dampen the twisting forces of its moving components. Not only did he solve the suspension problem, he discovered that such focused concentration led him to a deeper understanding of the washer's drive assembly—revelations that then led him to change the range of motion and force applied by the agitator that worked the load of clothing most efficiently.

He explained this transition to other revelations as "doors that led to other doors, behind which there are more ideas and solutions." Mentally entering "the room" always triggered a series of events in which problems were solved and answers were revealed, and those realizations led him to better understanding of an issue and future ideas and inventions.

Assuming that a particular state of mind was required to achieve such vivid and deep thought, we asked how he moved into a "room." He smiled and shook his head. "It really isn't anything special," he said, explaining that getting into a room was the result of a deliberate effort to get alone and consider a problem without distractions.

In the creative and improvement phases connected to landmark inventions such as CVap, he says it was helpful to seek the advice of likeminded peers who could discuss the nuances of problems in detail. "I would surround myself with people who could help me understand the science I was involved in," he says.

In some of his most productive years, time in "the room" came before sunrise at his kitchen table at home. Long before his family was out of bed, he made a pot of coffee and, with paper and pen in hand, he began thinking and sketching out his thoughts. Other times it was the reverse: him staying up late at night, often on vacation, when away from the distractions of the factory, and after his wife and children were asleep.

"I found myself constantly wrestling with new ideas, things which occupied my mind favorably," he says. "I never saw that as a burden since I knew that time thinking would lead to a positive outcome. I rather enjoyed that time alone."

Especially when it led to unintended consequences, such as the creation of CVap. Such eureka moments were startling and exciting, but often humbling, he says.

"When I finally understood the profound use of vapor as a heat transfer agent, I had to ask myself, 'How has this been missed by me and everybody else for so long?' I've never considered myself to be a better thinker than anybody else, and I'm frequently reminded that I'm not. But I do take the time to do it, to weigh the problem before me and work to arrive at a solution."

The discipline of putting himself in a room wasn't always easy. When imagining the design of a zero-turn mower in the 1960s, he was still employed at G.E. and had to do his thinking before the start of his hired work day. When his alarm sounded somewhere between 4 a.m. and 5 a.m., he often longed to stay in bed and rest a bit more, but he didn't allow it.

"Somedays it was easier than others, and some days I really had to push myself. I'd say to myself, 'Shelton, you know yesterday was a good day, and today likely will be, too. So, get your ass out of bed and get to work.'"

So now, we'll get out of the way and let Winston describe his visits to "the room" that led to the invention of CVap:

I consider all engineering a "room", and in that room, you solve problems and improve your product. You develop ideas on what your product should and can do, and inevitably, those ideas are applied to other things. That opens another door to other allied problems and inventions. If you approach the process methodically, you broaden your knowledge of the sciences that improve your position.

So, let's apply this to CVap. I wanted to hold food for extended periods at the ideal temperature that allowed it to be served quickly in a restaurant setting—and with the taste and texture of just being cooked! That food originally was the Colonel's fried chicken, which had to be moist on the inside yet have a fried exterior so it was, as he said, "Finger-lickin' good!"

That placed me in a room I would define as the Ovening Room, since the product had to be desirably hot. And since traditional holding cabinets are heated with dry heat, I considered the effect of that heat source on the food: it dried it out fairly quickly.

So, since the product in this room would be fried chicken, I extended that thought to create the notion of a "Best-Held Fried Chicken" room.

Then I started by asking myself, "What is food?" And the answer was that it's mostly water. Proteins are at least 75 percent moisture, while fruits and vegetables are between 80 and 95 percent water. That means I now have to be considerate of the moisture contained within the food if I'm going to hold it properly. Using dry heat only is not considerate of the fact that food is mostly water. To heat food with hot air, the food itself has to be dried out—have moisture evaporated from it—before you can actually heat it. That, of course, defeats the purpose because the food is no longer moist.

Now, still in the room, and now that I've defined the problem—which is that dry heat dries out food through moisture evaporation—I start discussing the problem with other engineers. And John Toma, an engineer from my G.E. days, asks me, "Winston, are you controlling wet bulb temperature?" (Wet bulb temperature is the temperature of air that is cooled to saturation by the evaporation of water into it. The measurement allows meteorologists to calculate relative humidity.) I admitted that I hadn't accounted for that. And he was correct, since food is a wet body, I had to account for wet bulb temperature to heat a wet body correctly.

So, I go back into the room and ask myself, "How can I heat food in such a manner that it won't lose its moisture?" The answer is water vapor or, perhaps wet heat or even humidity, such as the weatherman describes it.

So back inside the Best-Held Fried Chicken Room, when you heat water, it's axiomatic that the vapor pressure created will now surround the food and transfer its heat to the food. The vapor takes over and becomes the boss in that particular atmosphere, saying to the food, "I'm not going to let you evaporate your moisture. In fact, I'm going to lay some moisture on you to heat you and keep you moist."

I also know that when we heat this water, that vapor will search out every other thing in the room that has a lower vapor pressure, and when it finds them, it conveys its heat to those objects in an incredibly efficient way. Once you heat it and wet it, now the food has a vapor pressure, and every other surface in the room is now heated to the same temperature as the vapor.

So, by heating a pan of water in the oven, I could control the wet bulb temperature of the chicken—just by heating a pan of water at the bottom! Vapor became a volunteer heat-transfer agent that, unlike dry heat, maintained food moisture. When I realized that water vapor was what I needed to achieve my aim, I thought, "Why in the hell didn't somebody else do this before? How was this missed for so long?"

But if the oven also were to maintain the browned exterior of the fried chicken, it would be necessary to utilize heated air to maintain the texture of the chicken's surface. Therefore, that necessitated I control dry bulb temperature (dry bulb temperature is the temperature of air in the atmosphere) as well, which is achieved simply enough with electric heating elements placed within the oven. They would produce the dry heat. And controlling those dual heat sources precisely—while managing the temperature differential between them—would hold the chicken at optimal temperature and texture for extended periods.

As we began testing it, we saw how wonderfully it worked. I recall one test where I placed freshly fried chicken into the cabinet, set the wet and dry bulb temperatures and left for a meeting I thought would last one hour. When I came back three hours later, I was astonished to discover that the chicken was still succulent and crisp after such a long period of time.

As we tested it further, we were quite pleased to see how yield was vastly improved since the heated vapor kept the chicken from giving up its own moisture.

And from that simple realization, we learned many profound lessons—ideas that led to other "rooms" and solutions. Not only could this oven control food temperature precisely with water vapor, it also could cook food using water vapor at very low, but safe temperatures—far lower than steaming. Cooking food using vapor at such low temperatures increased yield significantly while achieving unparalleled succulence. You could cook an entire prime rib or top round of roast beef a perfect medium rare from top to bottom without the ring of discoloration near the meat's exterior so commonly associated with dry-heat cooking.

Gathering all these examples and a lot of data took me to another door inside the room: energy savings. Using water vapor to cook requires one-quarter of the energy of using dry heat. Vapor's energy intensity is about 20 times greater than air, so it's extremely efficient at transferring heat to another body; much more efficient than dry heat.

So, as I followed that, another door opened: that the device was labor saving because it cooked so precisely and without the chef's constant attention. It would allow the chef to put his foods in the oven, go shopping, go play with the kids and come back in several hours—and the food would be perfectly cooked to the temperatures set.

And much later, another door opened when I learned chefs were using CVap to cook their foods with vapor at very low, precise temperatures perfectly to a preselected endpoint of plus or minus a single degree! It was becoming clear to me that the technology had such phenomenal applications.

So, "the room" as we've called it, has a doorway in, but no doorway out. Going through the door only gives you access to the expansion of the science of other applications. Those doors for me, for example, were the building of a business that takes full advantage of vapor technology to expand its application to low-temperature pasteurization of foods, or to home air conditioning temperature sensors that sense wet bulb temperature rather than dry bulb—which is far more useful when trying to create real comfort. This science, or any science for that matter, developed to a great depth, produces additional doors to other sciences that build on those discovered in the first room.

That's where I was going at 4 in the morning. That's what I did in all the time I had during the day. That room that I synthesized confined me and my thinking to better understand all the benefits of the science of vapor technology, how to implement it, how to put it to work, and, of course, how to sell it.

Keep Innovating – Always!

I'd not be truthful if I told you I envisioned Winston Industries exactly as it is today: a thriving manufacturing company employing almost 200 team members and creating and manufacturing leading-edge foodservice equipment and electronic controls.

Believe me, when I left General Electric in 1969 to strike out with my brother, I had no idea that our company, Engineering Prototype Services, would evolve into the company it's since become.

Yet what I did know half a century ago was this: *I had the potential to change things, to make life better for others through innovation.*

Even at 95 years old, I still believe I possess that potential … when I walk inside my office every day … when I roll out of bed at night to sit before my computer to type out an idea that comes to mind… when a colleague sees something in my own designs that I've overlooked. The potential to innovate is always with us, and it's our responsibility to act on ideas that lead toward improvement.

A few essentials to innovation:

INNOVATING REQUIRES WORK, AND LOTS OF IT.

And I believe that work must be fulfilling, important and beneficial to others. Innovating for the sake of others is how we "pay our rent" for our time on Earth; it's how we give back to something that's given us so much.

Innovation requires courage and the willingness to make many mistakes along the way.

If one is concerned about being embarrassed by failure, you'll never innovate. You'll hide behind that fear and accept the status quo because it's comfortable.

INNOVATING REQUIRES A THICK SKIN.

For you can be certain that when sharing your ideas aloud, someone will always be waiting to criticize them. Such disapproval is hard enough to take when your ideas are truly wrong, but it's more difficult to accept when you're convinced you're right and the critics just don't see it. Or, worse, they refuse to accept it because it proves their ideas wrong. But forge ahead; don't give up!

Changing anything for the better is good and noble, especially when one has others' welfare in mind. Innovation may involve one, but it always should benefit all.

INNOVATION REQUIRES CHANGE, AND OFTEN CHANGE IS CONSIDERED TROUBLESOME.

Growing up, my parentss said I was prone to arguing about nearly everything with them and that I questioned them too often. I'm sure they were right, but to my defense, I was simply curious about the world. I asked lots of questions and questioned some of their long-held assumptions in order to figure things out.

Now nearly 96 years old, Winston still arrives every morning and works in the Advanced Engineering Lab at Winston Industries.

It's how I came to understand both the simple and the complex, and that mindset remains part of my nature.

In my pursuit to innovate as a G.E. engineer, I ruffled plenty of feathers, even when I did well. Often, I saw simple solutions to obvious problems that my colleagues—typically men far better educated than I—couldn't see or were embarrassed to admit they'd overlooked. I was certain others were bright enough to come up with the same solution as I, and perhaps they did. Yet they never shared it because they were embarrassed by the solution's simplicity. I'd solve a problem and think, "Well, that didn't take a Cambridge graduate to think of it. How could they miss it?"

It goes back to what I've referred to in this book as "sawmill engineering": a practical, hands-on understanding of how things work, which in turn gives a person the ability solve problems based on that life experience.

Another essential I've learned about innovation: it's more about correction and adjustment than pure invention.

The Mies pressure fryer I was asked to improve for Kentucky Fried Chicken was soundly designed except for its inability to filter its contents automatically. My innovation was to make it self-filtering by tapping into the fundamental forces of convective heat cycling and gravity. Though groundbreaking for its time, it wasn't an Earth-shattering discovery because it utilized very obvious forces of nature. But using those basic forces was innovative and highly effective, and four decades later, the Collectramatic Pressure Fryer is still Winston Industries' top-selling product. Save for the updated controls we now install to operate it, the Collectramatic is essentially the same cooker it's always been.

But CVap, the innovation that followed it, is another matter. We have yet to grasp its seemingly unlimited possibilities at Winston Industries, and our staff is constantly learning new ways to use it through the work of chefs experimenting with it across the world. Created as a temperature-controlled holding cabinet, we eventually discovered its greater value as an ovening device that cooks foods to precise temperatures and holds them safely in ready-to-eat condition for extraordinary lengths of time. And as amazing as that innovation is, it functions using the most basic of nature's provisions: water vapor. Life on Earth could not happen without it. Scientists claim that without our moisture-laden atmosphere, the daytime temperature of the Earth would soar to well over 400°F. But it doesn't because that ever-present and invisible water vapor never stops absorbing and regulating the sun's heat. Using that same vapor to cook and hold food is, for now, my greatest innovation, and I'm still conceiving many possible applications of Controlled Vapor Technology.

After three decades of use in foodservice, CVap's simple operation is well proven. I believe that what works well for the world's finest chefs can work for the average home cook. It's truly that simple to master. So, now the charge before us is to make it smaller and more elegant for use in the home. (Frankly, I love its industrial look, but as my colleagues tell me regularly, those who aren't engineers probably don't find stainless steel and digital control panels quite so appealing.)

In the company's early days, I hired good people who, in turn, hired other good people, and that quality of employees has ratcheted upward to the point that we now have the best people on our team that the company has ever had. And as an employer, it makes me realize that they place their livelihood in my hands, which is a profound thought that humbles and leads me to resolve to do even better work for their sake.

In August of 2010, management of the company passed from David to Valerie. As it has grown, Winston Industries has become far more than a manufacturer of Collectramatics and CVaps. As I developed both machines, I insisted we manufacture our own controls. Not only was that a quality decision, it ensured we kept a few of our secrets to ourselves. However, Valerie pointed out several years ago that the expense of keeping such a labor-intensive part of our business for two appliance lines made little fiscal sense. When a discussion of outsourcing our controls needs began, it actually became a conversation about creating a new business that could make high-quality controls for other firms that lacked the infrastructure to make their own. We had the know-how and the equipment, so why not make controls for others?

In October of 2012, Valerie recruited Teri McDonald and a new division named Win2uit was born. By the end of 2013, Win2uit had moved into our building at 2349 Carton Drive, become ISO certified, and achieved revenue approaching $300,000. And now as 2017 draws to a close, Win2uit produced over $5M in outside sales and produced another $3M in product for other divisions in the company.

Valerie and her management team continued to grow the business by establishing two more divisions: the Manufacturing Division which markets our excess manufacturing capacity to businesses across America, and the Ventures Division which resembles that of my Engineering Prototype Services business years ago. They have also brought new technology into several areas of the business.

Recently, I visited our manufacturing operation and was astonished to watch some of the machines we have and the highly skilled people we have operating them. We've come so far from the days when we assembled Collectramatics mostly by hand, to now, when a single machine can do a variety of tasks that I'd have never imagined. Such advances give me great joy. Several years ago, we decided that newer and more automated machinery was required to match the pace of increasing demand for our products, and in 2013 we made a multi-million-dollar equipment investment. Seeing those new machines make our products with such increased speed led us to see we also could manufacture goods for other firms that lacked our expertise and infrastructure. That led to the creation of a fabrication and design service division that serves other companies whose needs matched our capabilities. Like Win2uit, that division of our company is also enjoying exceptional growth and revenue gains.

Taking it all in is a bit of a challenge for me—a boy of a humble upbringing in the Appalachian Mountains of West Virginia. I loved where I grew up, and I'm proud to the core of my family's heritage. Outside of my old stomping grounds, however, I learned the hard way that not everyone thinks so much of people from that area.

Once, while in the Army and stationed at Princeton University, a couple of people in my unit—big city guys who didn't see me as their cultural equal—did their best to insult me about where I'd come from. Their antagonism over the issue increased to the point that I told both of them that someone would end up with a broken nose if they didn't cut it out. When I made clear that I wasn't afraid to demonstrate the way West Virginians sometimes settled their differences, they relented. During my time at G.E. I endured similar remarks from other professionals.

My point isn't to engage in self-pity, for all of us, at one time or another, has to endure such senseless negativity from others. My purpose in recalling those experiences is to demonstrate how one's roots—despite another's perception of their worth—are often invaluable in the service of what we can become. In other words, I dare say those guys would look at Winston Industries and say that my upbringing was a detriment.

And so, I encourage you also to ignore the naysayers standing along the sidelines during your journey toward innovation. Resolve to regard your past, present and future as essential and beneficial to what you can become, what you can create and to how you can innovate to benefit others.

I admit that at that tense moment back at Princeton, my sense of innovation centered on rearranging those boys' looks. Yet 70 years later, I view it as just another test I had to pass to become a believer in my own self-worth and understanding of what I could become. It steeled me for the challenges that lay ahead. When you dare to innovate, I can assure you that both your ideas and your grit will be challenged.

My vision for Winston Industries was always that it would be a great company, but for the most part, my ability to envision its future realistically amounted to only the next step or two. It took others to make it grow, bright, talented and hardworking people who managed far more together than I could do on my own. To innovate effectively, one must collaborate and rely on the strengths of others.

Without the hundreds of other folks who've worked at Winston Industries in the past and many of whom remain on board today, the success I've enjoyed would not have happened. I'd merely be one engineer with a lot of great ideas. And it's to this team that I owe a great debt of gratitude.

Innovate constantly and fearlessly!

– Winston Shelton, 2018